THE BATTLE OF
BRITAIN
POCKET MANUAL 1940

Edited by Chris McNab

CASEMATE
Oxford & Philadelphia

Published in Great Britain and
the United States of America in 2020 by
CASEMATE PUBLISHERS
The Old Music Hall, 106–108 Cowley Road, Oxford OX4 1JE, UK
1950 Lawrence Road, Havertown, PA 19083, USA

Introduction and chapter introductory texts by Chris McNab
© Casemate Publishers 2020

Hardback Edition: ISBN 978-1-61200-869-1
Digital Edition: ISBN 978-1-61200-870-7

A CIP record for this book is available from the British Library

Printed and bound in India by Replika Press Pvt. Ltd.

Typeset by Versatile PreMedia Services (P) Ltd

The information contained in the documents in this book is solely for historical interest
and does not constitute advice. The publisher accepts no liability for the consequences of
following any of the details in this book.

For a complete list of Casemate titles, please contact:

CASEMATE PUBLISHERS (UK)
Telephone (01865) 241249
Fax (01865) 794449
Email: casemate-uk@casematepublishers.co.uk
www.casematepublishers.co.uk

CASEMATE PUBLISHERS (US)
Telephone (610) 853-9131
Fax (610) 853-9146
Email: casemate@casematepublishers.com
www.casematepublishers.com

Front cover illustration by Grayson Hanchin

CONTENTS

INTRODUCTION

By the summer of 1940, Britain's government and citizens were braced for the worst. When World War II began in September 1939, with German's invasion of Poland and Britain's almost immediate declaration of war, the Nazi juggernaut was half a continent away from the British mainland. Western Europe provided, as it had in the previous world war, a territorial buffer zone for the British people and government, not least because the invasion and occupation of Poland were largely followed by six months of relative inactivity, labelled as the 'Phoney War'. Few could have envisaged how everything would change in the spring of 1940. Beginning with the German invasion of Scandinavia on 9 April, and followed by a vast *Blitzkrieg* drive through France, the Netherlands, Luxembourg and Belgium from 10 May, by 20 May the Wehrmacht (German armed forces) armoured and infantry formations had reached the Channel coast. By 4 June, the last weary remnants of the British Expeditionary Force (BEF) were evacuated back to Britain, the success of the evacuation rather masking the epic scale of the defeat in mainland Europe, and on 22 June the French authorities signed an armistice. Britain was now, truly, alone. The only question that seemed to be on every British citizen's mind was, when would their turn come to be invaded by an apparently unstoppable Germany?

Operation *Sealion*

In July 1940, Hitler had already authorised preparations for *Unternehmen Seelöwe* (Operation *Sealion*), the invasion of the UK, but this action would be unlike any other the Wehrmacht had performed to date. The chief obstacle was that relatively thin sliver of water, the English Channel, which at its narrowest point separated occupied France from England by just 33km (20.7 miles). The German plan to land two entire armies along England's south-eastern coastline would necessarily be an amphibious operation, and in this regard the Wehrmacht faced two major defensive obstacles. The first was the Royal Navy, still the most powerful of the world's navies, which could potentially wreck an amphibious force as it made its crossing. The second was the Royal Air Force (RAF), whose bombers and fighters could also prey upon an invasion fleet. RAF airpower had a further tactical application in that it could provide the Royal Navy with top cover against anti-shipping strikes by the Luftwaffe (German Air Force).

It was therefore clear to Hitler that a condition of *Sealion*'s success was the pre-emptive subjugation of the RAF. To this end, he tasked Reichsmarschall Hermann Göring, the head of the Luftwaffe, with the neutralisation of Britain's air force, an objective that the bullish Göring heartily and confidently embraced. Here were the seeds of the Battle of Britain.

Although the precipitous collapse of Western Europe to the Nazis had certainly shocked the British in 1940, the prospect of a potential German invasion, and the importance of air power in resisting it, had been considered within weeks of the war beginning in 1939. A government document dated 29 October 1939, entitled 'Measures to be taken to ensure co-ordination of action in the event of a German invasion of England', took a rational look at how the Luftwaffe might be used to support an invasion, and equally how the RAF would resist it. The following passage provides some useful context:

COURSE OPEN TO THE ENEMY

Air Superiority essential

3. It is unnecessary to emphasise the extreme vulnerability of air attack of transports, landing boats and beaches and of transport aircraft. A successful invasion by sea or air is out of the question in the face of the full strength of our air striking and defence forces. Germany has tested our air defences and found them to be effective even at some distance from our coasts. She is not therefore likely to attempt invasion until she has obtained complete mastery of these defences and followed it up with an offensive against our Striking Force with the object of completely neutralising it.

Method of attaining air superiority.

4. The essential preparatory air offensive might take one of two forms:–
(a) Extended operations against our air potential – industry, reserves, aerodromes and first-line aircraft.
(b) a sudden and concentrated offensive, in the period immediately prior to the invasion, against our first-line fighter, bomber and T.B. stations.

Regarding option (a), the author of the document goes on to rather complacently state that 'These have been appreciated and our A.A. [anti-aircraft] defences have been deployed to meet the threat.' For point (b), he identifies three possible courses of action for the Luftwaffe:

(i) A night attack against all fighter stations with bombs and gas and possibly with sabotage parties either landed on aerodromes or parachuted. [. . .]
(ii) An attack against all bombers stations at the critical time of the invasion – probably dawn following the landing. [. . .]
(iii) A general and sustained offensive against all first-line aerodromes on the day of the landing with the object of keeping bombers out of the air and containing the fighters.

As it happened, the Luftwaffe would not put all its eggs in one basket, attempting to dominate the RAF on the day of the invasion. Instead, it would opt for an extended campaign designed around two main objectives:

- bombing raids against both naval and aviation ground targets, e.g. ports, airfields, aircraft manufacturing plants etc., to destabilise the logistical framework on both the RAF and the Navy in the south.
- drawing the RAF, particularly fighter forces in southern England, into destructive air-to-air engagements by bombing British shipping passing through the English Channel and by hitting southern towns and cities, including London.

Thus we see something of a mismatch between the expectations of the air war in 1939, and that which actually unfolded between July and September 1940 over the skies of Britain. Strategically, the RAF had to a large degree considered its defence in terms of long-range bomber counter-offensives, rather than short-range fighter combat enacted in British airspace. As it soon became clear in the summer of 1940, Britain's potential survival depended upon a collection of single-seat monoplane fighters, and the men who flew them, pitted against a Luftwaffe riding high on the confidence of victory.

Phases of the Battle

The Battle of Britain does not have sharply cut start and end dates. Classically, the battle is said to have lasted from about 10 July to 15 September, although the last date can be convincingly argued into late October, and the start date might be pushed back into the previous month. For our purposes, however, just a basic overview of the contours of the battle will set the scene for what is to follow.

Small-scale *Störangriffe* ('nuisance raids') began over Britain in June 1940, with minor bombing raids conducted in both daylight and at night. These were not sizeable raids, but they gave the Luftwaffe initial operational insight into British air defences; conversely, they also gave RAF Fighter Command experience of raid detection, interception and air combat tactics. Yet most historians class the battle proper as beginning with the *Kanalkampf* (Channel Battle), which escalated during the first two weeks of July and lasted until 11 August. During this period, Luftwaffe bombers, flying with heavy fighter escort, bombed British shipping passing through the Channel, plus important southern ports, attacks that brought out the RAF in a protective response. Soon the skies over and around the Channel waters roared to the sound of aero engines at full throttle, and the rippling sound of machine guns. Aerial losses were heavy on both sides during this phase: one calculation places the casualties at 215 Luftwaffe aircraft destroyed for 115 RAF aircraft. These figures, however, reflect a tactical imbalance – 80 of the Luftwaffe aircraft destroyed were fighters (53 Bf 109s and 27 Bf 110s), while *all* the RAF aircraft were fighter types, the majority Hurricanes and Spitfires.

But despite the RAF combat losses, it was quickly evident to the Luftwaffe that the RAF was neither running out of aircraft nor succumbing to any sort of defeatism, and that the British aviators were consistently managing to inflict serious losses on the German air fleets. On 12 August, therefore, a new strategy was implemented, bringing about the third phase of the battle. Now the target was the RAF in the most direct fashion – heavy bombing raids conducted against RAF airfields in southern England, plus attacks on air-defence radar installations, all with bristling fighter escort. Indeed, as this phase progressed, the Luftwaffe deliberately scaled down the numbers of bombers on daylight raids – their role now mainly to serve as bait – and scaled up the numbers of fighters, in a direct effort to wipe out Fighter Command in the air.

For the Germans, this phase of the battle, which also included unescorted night-bombing raids on British industrial targets, technically began on 13 August with *Adlertag* (Eagle Day), the opening massed air battle of *Unternehmen Adlerangriff* (Operation *Eagle Attack*). (Note that for most German historians, this phase is what they classically regard as the Battle of Britain.) The action was certainly punishing – the British lost 13 fighters in the air and 47 on the ground, while the Luftwaffe air losses were 47–48 aircraft. In fact, this was the period that stretched Fighter Command almost to breaking point. The biggest challenge lay not in finding replacement aircraft, which British industry was churning out at levels to meet the losses, but rather in finding replacement trained pilots, who couldn't be made to order in a factory.

But throughout August and into September, much to Göring's frustrated anger, the RAF appeared to be undaunted and undiminished, and continued to send appreciable volumes of his aircraft down in flames on a daily basis. Furthermore, by late August Hitler's commitment to *Sealion* was beginning to drain away anyway, as his focus had by now turned eastwards, towards the future invasion of the Soviet Union. Invading Britain began to appear increasingly impractical and unnecessary. In September, therefore, came a signal change in the focus of the German air campaign. On 7 September, the Luftwaffe launched a series of mass bombing raids on London, hitting the dockyards and industrial areas with the ordnance of nearly 400 bombers. Although the raid had copious fighter escort – the bombers were accompanied by more than 600 fighters – the principal objective was the destruction wrought on the city. It was the beginning of what we now know as the 'Blitz', a concerted attempt to bomb Britain's infrastructure and civilian population into submission, mainly through the vehicle of night raids.

This campaign, which lasted until May 1941 in its first iteration, plus subsequent smaller bombing campaigns until 1944, would kill some 60,000 of Britain's civilian population. It did, however, start to give RAF Fighter Command breathing space to recover; had Göring persisted with the *Adlerangriff* for a few more months, the outcome of the Battle of Britain might have been quite different. The first two weeks of September still saw major air-to-air engagements over southern England. Indeed, they culminated in what we today call 'Battle of Britain Day' – 15 September – when a huge armada of German bombers and fighters (the former heading for London) clashed over southern England, in what Göring hoped would be a final catastrophic blow for the RAF and the restoration of his dwindling reputation. Some 1,500 aircraft clashed, but when the final tallies were counted it was the Luftwaffe, once again, who had come off worse, losing up to 61 aircraft for 29 RAF fighters destroyed. For Hitler, this defeat was the final signal that *Sealion* was no long viable, and two days later he indefinitely postponed the invasion of Britain, a strategic decision that in many ways directly contributed to the final defeat of Nazi Germany in 1945.

Winston Churchill famously said of the debt Britain's people owed the RAF fighter pilots: 'Never in the field of human conflict was so much owed by so many to so few.' As we shall see in this book, that undeniably affirmative statement hides some factual distortions that embedded themselves in post-war popular history, but the core of its sentiment is accurate. Had not hundreds of young men hurled themselves into the air and literally fought to the death over England, then the history of Britain and the outcome of the war itself might have steered themselves in very different directions.

The book brings together numerous primary sources to explore both the RAF and the Luftwaffe as organisations during the Battle of Britain, and how the battle was fought practically in the skies. A major part of the book is devoted, quite naturally, to the tactics and outcomes of the air combat. Yet here we also explore the RAF as a wider entity, the focus not just restricted to the 'tip of the spear' – the few hundred fighter pilots – but also to the tens of thousands of personnel in the wider organisation, all of whom made their own contribution to victory.

CHAPTER I
OPPOSING FORCES

A popular understanding of the Battle of Britain usually represents the British as 'the few', heavily outnumbered by the Luftwaffe and always on the brink of their endurance. Certainly the last point is true from a human perspective, but in reality the two forces were, in practical combat terms, quite evenly balanced. RAF Fighter Command, headed by Air Chief Marshal Hugh Dowding, had roughly 900 fighter aircraft available by the beginning of July 1940, the majority of these being modern Hurricanes and Spitfires (weighted heavily towards the former), plus far smaller numbers of Blenheims and Defiants. The main German *Luftflotten* (Air Fleets) arraigned against them across the Channel and North Sea – Luftflotten 2, 3 and 5 – between them had about 1,080 modern fighters, although 280 of these were twin-engine Messerschmitt Bf 110s. The air fleets would also bring a large number of light and medium bombers (Heinkel He 111 and Dornier Do 17, plus the Ju 88 multirole bomber). These would, of course, pull the attention of the RAF fighters' efforts, but on a fighter vs. fighter basis, the RAF and the Luftwaffe were largely peer competitors, not least when some of the Luftwaffe's disadvantages were factored in, especially limitations in range of operation. (The Bf 109s had very limited loiter time over Britain before being compelled to turn for home because of lack of fuel.) British production figures for combat aircraft also exceeded expectations in May–October 1940, by some significant margins. For example, in July it was expected that total production of Spitfires and Hurricanes would be 329 aircraft, but by the end of the month 496 had been manufactured. Similar beneficial disparities would be seen in all the months of the battle, helping the RAF keep pace with its combat losses.

Our first source, one volume of the two-part *Royal Air Force War Manual*, explains the overall general structure of the RAF at this time, in terms of its unit composition and chain of command. The first paragraphs, however, explore the general qualities of the service, qualities that surely contributed towards the eventual British victory by the autumn of 1940.

From *Royal Air Force War Manual, Part 2, Organization and Administration*, 2nd edition (1940)

INTRODUCTION.

1. Under the modern conditions in which fighting services are called upon to operate, victory inclines to the force which is most thoroughly and efficiently organized.

2. The Royal Air Force is a highly specialised fighting service with elaborate and costly equipment, dispersed widely over the world and subject to changes of location and activities. It strives in peace to fit itself for the exacting duties of war. It may be called upon to fight with an abrupt transition from a peace to a war footing. During war the only certainty is that an enemy will endeavour to hamper and nullify every effort which it makes. To meet these requirements the Royal Air Force requires a basic organization and a system of administration which will enable its individuals to apply with courage, foresight and common sense, the material resources at their disposal to defeat the enemy.

3. An organization is a composite body the constituent parts of which are required to work together for a common purpose. Having decided upon the purpose for which an organization is required, two things have to be done to bring it into being. A suitable number and type of constituent parts have to be designed, and these have then to be brought into interdependent relations so as to form and to be capable of action as one organic whole.

4. A great number of constituent parts, or units, are necessary in any great organization. In the Royal Air Force these are divided into headquarters units and operational and administrative units. Each operational or administrative unit has its own commander and these units are normally grouped together for a common purpose under the control of a higher commander, who is given a headquarters unit to enable him to exercise his command.

5. The organization of the Royal Air Force must be constantly adapted and perfected as the result of experience and must be capable of conforming to the demands of the situation at the time and the needs of technical progress.

6. An organization may be compared with a machine. Both possess components which have to be designed in relation to other components to perform a specific function in order that the machine as a whole may do its work efficiently. But the best results can only be obtained from a perfect machine if it is well handled. This applies equally to an organization. A good organization requires competent

management to produce satisfactory results. In the Royal Air Force this management of the organization is called administration and is the system whereby, in principle and in executive detail, the Service carries out its functions and is able to operate efficiently.

7. The administration of the Royal Air Force is entrusted to the personnel comprising the force. Each member in a greater or less degree has his own responsibility for controlling activities within his allotted sphere.

Important Features or Characteristics of an Organization

8. The successful functioning of an organization depends to a considerable extent upon its possessing certain important features or characteristics.

Unity of Direction

9. An organization is created to fulfil a specific purpose. Unity of direction is essential for ensuring concentration of effort upon that purpose. Concentration of effort, in turn, depends upon each component of the organization receiving precise instructions to enable it to know what action is required of it to assist the whole body to achieve the selected aim. Moreover, unity of direction is essential to ensure, as the situation changes or as new situations arise, that precise and co-ordinated instructions are issued at once to all concerned.

A squadron of Boulton Paul Defiant interceptors readies for take-off.

Decentralisation of Responsibility and Authority

10. In order that the decisions made by the supreme directing authority may be turned into appropriate action by the components of an organization it is necessary to establish subordinate controlling elements at various levels throughout the structure of an organization. To ensure an even distribution of stress throughout the organization responsibility and authority have to be decentralised to an appropriate degree to each of the subordinate controlling elements. By so doing each controlling element, from the highest to the lowest, bears its proper share of the work entailed in controlling and supervising the activities of the organization. It is important that decentralisation of responsibility should be accompanied by a proportionate decentralisation of authority.

11. The extent to which responsibility and authority is delegated to each subordinate controlling element, and the degree of detail with which it will have to deal, will depend upon its level within the organization.

12. In the Royal Air Force these controlling elements are known as headquarters units. The maximum amount of work that any one headquarters unit can efficiently discharge is limited. If this limit is exceeded, efficiency will be lowered. For maximum efficiency, therefore, the number of subordinate headquarters will have carefully to be selected. It follows from this that if any headquarters fails to discharge all its allotted responsibilities and allows some of them to pass to the next higher headquarters the latter will be dealing with a greater volume of work and possibly in a greater degree of detail than it was designed to undertake. It will thus become overstressed and will constitute a source of weakness. Except in an emergency, it is equally undesirable for a headquarters to exceed the responsibilities delegated to it, because this tends to destroy the proper distribution of responsibility throughout the organization. In an emergency, when there is no time to refer to higher authority, a junior headquarters must, of course, be prepared to use initiative, and, if necessary, to make decisions even if such decisions exceed the responsibility normally delegated to the headquarters concerned. But it must inform the appropriate higher authority as soon as possible regarding the action it has taken.

13. A natural corollary to the decentralisation of responsibility and authority is the need for a clear definition of responsibility at every level within a military organization. This is necessary to enable subordinate headquarters to know what matters are appropriate to their level and to know what matters they should pass on to be dealt with by higher authority.

Co-operation

14. Co-operation is essential to ensure speed, economy and efficiency of working. Every component of an organization may exert itself to the full towards a common

end, but unless each component has a sufficient appreciation of the functions, capabilities and limitations of the others with which it is closely associated, wasted effort is bound to result for reasons such as overlapping, failure to lend assistance when needed, failure to apply for assistance to the right quarter when needed, or failure to take action in the belief that it should be or is being taken by some other component. Co-operation can only result from sound leadership together with carefully thought out instructions from superior authorities and from the intelligent application of these instructions by subordinate authorities, who have a knowledge of the functions, capabilities and limitations of the other components with which they are required to work in the course of discharging their duties.

15. Co-operation is, therefore, not something that can be mechanically created in the same way as formations can be created by grouping units together. Co-operation requires a desire on the part of all members of a service to know their own jobs well and to know sufficient of those of others to be able to work harmoniously together. Co-operation is something that comes from within a service, and to which every member of a service contributes.

Co-ordination

16. Co-ordination is essential in a fighting service to enable it to develop the greatest potential effort of which it is capable at the right time and in the right direction. Co-ordination emanates not from within the body as does co-operation, but from the directing authorities, which arrange the type and timing of individual efforts so as best to meet situations as they arise.

Flexibility

17. However well an organization may be suited to meet a particular situation, it would not meet the requirements of an air force unless it possessed the characteristic of flexibility. Flexibility in a military organization is the quality which imparts the ability to make quick and smooth adjustments to meet stresses thrown upon it by varying and unforeseen circumstances.

18. The degree to which an organization is flexible depends not only upon the structure of the organization, but also upon the ability of those who administer it. They must have a thorough appreciation both of the purposes for which the organization was created and of the functions which each component was designed to fulfil. They must study the structure of the organization, with particular reference to the links connecting the various components. They must be capable of recognising new situations when they arise and they must be capable of adapting the organization to meet the demands of these new situations.

Initiative and Responsibility

19. The encouragement of initiative and of the desire for responsibility is a most necessary feature in an organization, but here, as in many other things, a careful balance has to be struck. In decentralising responsibility and providing scope for initiative great care has to be taken not to endanger unity of command. The extent to which a commander can achieve this is one of the great tests of his ability.

20. It is to the commander and his headquarters unit that all the other units of a formation look for direction, guidance and assistance in carrying out their tasks, particularly in times of stress. The excellence or otherwise of the work of the headquarters is thus reflected throughout the formation. Much, therefore, depends upon the ability and the efficiency of the policy staff and the staffs of the services in a headquarters. It is essential for all concerned to have a knowledge of the structure of the organization of the Royal Air Force and of the machinery that is put at their disposal for controlling its many and complex components. In particular it is most important for all senior policy staff officers and chiefs of the services to instil into their subordinates a thorough grasp of the principles upon which the organization of the Royal Air Force is based and the manner in which the machinery of the headquarters organization should be used in order to obtain full efficiency from it.

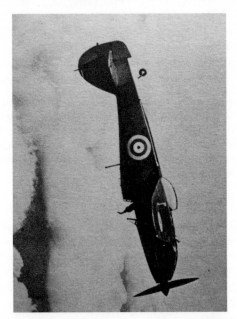

A Hawker Hurricane performs an aerial combat manoeuvre.

CHAPTER I
THE ORGANIZATION OF THE ROYAL AIR FORCE

Section I—The Structure of the Organization
Operating Conditions Organization designed to meet

1. The organization with which this manual deals is that for air forces operating under one or more of the following conditions:—

(i) In defence of the United Kingdom with air force operating from air stations in the United Kingdom.

(ii) In the defence of possessions overseas and of Imperial communications, with air forces operating from air stations in one or more of the existing overseas commands.

(iii) As air forces detached from either the United Kingdom or one or more of the existing overseas commands and operating from air stations in allied territory or in parts of the Empire not normally occupied by air forces in times of peace. In these circumstances air forces may be engaged in air operations,

(a) under an air force commander in a theatre where no military forces are operating.

(b) under an air force commander but in conjunction with Naval and/or Army forces under their respective commanders.

(iv) As the air force component of an army field force. In these circumstances the air forces will be subordinate to the military officer in command.

2. The organization described in this manual is designed to meet many different situations and cannot, therefore, be rigid in all its details. It has been drawn up to meet normal rather than exceptional circumstances. There may, therefore, be occasions when some modification is necessary. But any modification to suit exceptional circumstances must not constitute a departure from the principles upon which the organization is based.

The Composition of Air Forces

3. In addition to headquarters units, upon whose establishments commanders, their staffs and their assistants are borne, an air force is made up of the following type of units:—

(i) Squadrons—*i.e.* fighting units.
(ii) Maintenance units—Technical and nontechnical.
(iii) Training units—Flying and non-flying.
(iv) Medical units.
(v) Other units with special functions.

Squadrons

4. The squadrons are equipped with fighter, bomber, reconnaissance, or other aircraft, the characteristics and functions of which are given in the War Manual Part I.

5. Squadrons are sub-divided into flights and sections. A typical squadron may contain two or three flying flights and a headquarters flight. In addition to the squadron headquarters, the headquarters flight may contain certain other sections such as the armament section, the photographic section, and the M.T. section. On the other hand, when two or more non-mobile squadrons exist on the same station, the M.T. section, W/T section, workshops section, etc., usually serve both squadrons and are organized as sections directly under the station headquarters. This also applies to mobile two squadron wings.

6. Besides being grouped together to form wings or stations, squadrons may have to operate separately, in which event they are provided with a suitable operational and administrative headquarters.

Maintenance Units

7. The storage, issue and, where applicable, the repair of all classes of equipment, stores, fuel and explosives required by the air force is undertaken by the maintenance units. Maintenance units may also be responsible for salvage work which is beyond the capacity of the fighting units.

8. The function of any particular maintenance unit may either be purely storage or purely repair, or in some instances both. The internal organization of each maintenance unit is arranged to suit its particular requirements.

Training Units

9. The operation and maintenance of an air force requires personnel with expert knowledge of a great variety of subjects and skilled in many trades.

10. The work of providing these experts and skilled tradesmen, including the pilots and aircraft crews, is undertaken in the training units of the Royal Air Force.

11. Details of the internal organization of training units are beyond the scope of this manual, owing to the many different types of internal organization that exist to meet the special requirements of each class of unit.

Medical Units

12. The medical units of the air force fall into two categories. There are the permanent air force hospitals and research institutions in the United Kingdom and in the commands overseas. There are also the medical units which are included in a

field force. The functions and organization of these medical units are dealt with in later chapters of this manual.

Units With Special Duties

13. There are various units with special duties in an air force which include balloon barrage squadrons, armoured car units and experimental establishments.

Allocation of Units to Air Force Formations

14. The proportion of each type of unit allotted to any specific air force formation depends upon the nature of the responsibilities of the formation. This proportion is subject to continuous review in peace time as to its suitability to meet a war situation. The war composition may be dependent upon appropriate reinforcement schemes.

Air Force Formations

15. The basis of any organization is the system whereby the main formation controls the activities of a number of subordinate formations. The number of subordinate formations which can conveniently and efficiently be controlled by a main formation is usually three or four. This number, however, varies and depends upon such factors as whether the characteristics and functions of the subsidiary formations are similar or different; upon the geographical situation of the subordinate formations; upon the facilities for communication and upon the type of control that has to be exercised. An intermediate formation is normally only interposed where the number of junior formations or units becomes too unwieldy or where they are dispersed too widely for them to be controlled and administered efficiently by a single senior formation.

16. The formations into which air force units are organised are:—
   Commands
   Groups
   Wings or stations.

Commands

17. There is no fixed rule regarding the number or type of formations in a command. A large command may contain from three to six groups, while in a small command there may be no groups at all, wings or even squadrons being controlled direct from command headquarters.

Groups

18. Groups control a number of wings, stations or units. The number is not fixed and may vary considerably. Units are usually controlled by groups through the

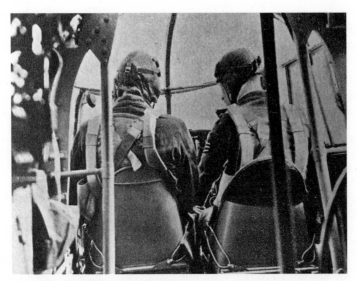

In the cockpit of an Airspeed dual-control instructional machine.

medium of wing or station headquarters, though in some circumstances they may be controlled directly from the group.

Wings

19. When formations composed of squadrons grouped together under a single controlling headquarters are on a mobile basis, they are called wings, so as to enable the identity of the formations to be retained irrespective of frequent changes of locality.

Stations

20. When units (either headquarters, fighting or of any other nature) are assembled together they are normally, for the purposes of convenience, described as a station. The Royal Air Force stations necessarily vary greatly in size and in the number and type of units which they contain. On any station much work has to be undertaken in connection with the administration and local organization of the station and with providing for the domestic needs of the units, which can be separated and kept distinct from the operational or other primary functions of the units on the station. Work of this nature is known as station administration and involves such matters as fire regulations, quarters, messing, upkeep of buildings, etc., which are more or less common to all stations irrespective of size or of the number and type of units on the station.

21. Every station has an officer appointed as station commander, and upon this officer devolves the responsibility for station administration. The station commander is provided with a number of assistants who form the station headquarters. His principal assistant is known as the "Station Administrative Officer" (S.Ad.O.).

22. Besides being responsible for all matters of station administration, the station commander, on the majority of stations, also controls the operations and/or training of the units on his station and is responsible to the next higher formation (group or command according to circumstance) for their efficiency. Thus, for example, a station on which there are two bomber squadrons is the equivalent of a wing, with the station commander fulfilling the functions of the commander of the wing, and with the station headquarters as the wing headquarters.

A station is not, however, always the equivalent of a wing. In some instances, it may contain several wings, while in others it may contain units (schools, colleges, training centres) which do not come under the control of the station commander. In the latter event, the station headquarters is not a link in the chain of control between the units on the station and higher formations, and the station commander has no operational responsibility, but is merely charged with the administration of the station.

23. Station commanders, who have considerable operational and training responsibilities, should delegate to the Station Administrative Officer as much of the work in connection with the administrative routine of the station and the direction of the administrative services on the station as they consider necessary to allow them to devote adequate time to operational and training matters.

Hawker Hurricanes flying in formation.

Chapter 1. Opposing Forces

The Luftwaffe was one of the central pillars of German *Blitzkrieg* (literally 'lightning war') tactics, particularly in its applications as aerial artillery. The following source is from the *Handbook of the German Air Force*, an Air Ministry publication published just months before the beginning of World War II in September 1939. It explains some of the basic organisational divisions of the Luftwaffe, down to what, in the RAF, would be squadron level. It is worth mentioning, however, that this neat description belies some of the inefficiencies and complexities at the top of the Luftwaffe's chain of command. Göring, as the Reich aviation minister, presided over a confused upper hierarchy through the Reichsluftfahrtministerium (Reich Aviation Ministry), with the office of Secretary of State for Air headed by Erhard Milch (also the Inspector-General of the Luftwaffe) frequently wrestling for authority with the Luftwaffe Chief of Staff Hans Jeschonnek and the Luftwaffe's technical office, headed by General Ernst Udet.

From *Handbook of the German Air Force* (July 1939)

CHAPTER 2
CONSTITUTION

1. The German Air Force, like the Army and the Navy, is constituted as a separate arm of the Defence Services. It is administered by an Air Ministry and, along with the two older services, comes under the supreme control of Herr Hitler who is advised by a staff made up from all three services called the OBERKOMMANDO der WEHRMACHT. The Air Force includes all German Anti-Aircraft Artillery with the exception of ships' guns and a few guns mounted in coastal forts which are manned by the Navy.

2. All Army and Naval air requirements are met by the Air Ministry.

3. Unlike the Royal Air Force the German Air Force is composed of the several different Branches, Corps, etc., shown below:–

> Flying Branch.
> Anti-Aircraft Artillery.
> Signals Corps.
> Engineer Corps.
> Parachute Troops.
> Air Landing Troops.
> General Goering Regiment.
> Air Police.

4. In addition the German Air Ministry controls every aspect of civil and commercial aviation to a degree which can only be achieved under a dictatorship. It is also responsible for all measures of passive air defence.

General

1. The German Air Force is organised on a territorial basis. There are four Commands called Air Fleets (LUFTFLOTTEN) and one major frontier air defence Command known as the LUFTVERTEIDIGUNGSKOMMANDO WEST. [. . .] Within the Luftflotten Commands the majority of operational units, with the exception of home defence fighters, Army Co-operation, and Coastal Reconnaissance units, are grouped into Air Divisions (FLIEGER DIVISIONEN). These Air Divisions are mobile formations and constitute Germany's striking force. The area within each Luftflotte is divided into smaller areas called LUFTGAUE. Luftgau Commanders are responsible for training, administration, and internal air defence except for frontier areas covered by an independent Air Defence Command.

CHAPTER 3, SECTION 2
ORGANIZATION – FORMATIONS AND FLYING UNITS

General

1. German operational formations and flying units are grouped as follows:—

Geschwader = a formation of 2 – 4 Gruppen

Gruppe = a unit of 3 – 4 Staffeln

Staffel = a unit of 12 – 18 aircraft

Geschwader

2. A Geschwader is a mobile formation commanded normally by a Colonel or Lieut Colonel who has a small Air Staff. It has its own Headquarters Flight of three aircraft of the same type of aircraft with which its Units are armed. Geschwader are homogeneous formations but may have other units attached to them. Their size may vary as follows: —

Bomber Geschwader   – 3 or 4 (B) GRUPPEN

Fighter "   – 2 or 3 (F)   "

A (B) Geschwader has, normally, one Long Reconnaissance Staffel attached to it.

Gruppen

3. A Gruppe is commanded by a Lieut Colonel or Major assisted by one or two staff officers. It generally occupies one station, the Commander also becoming the Station Commander. Like the Geschwader Headquarters it is mobile and has its own Flight. Gruppen contain a varying number of Staffeln (a mixture between a British Squadron and Flight) and, with the exception of those comprised of Reconnaissance or Coastal Units, are homogeneous.

A Gruppe may consist of:–

(B) Gruppe	3 (B) Staffeln
(F) "	3 (F) "
(R) "	3 or 4 Long and short Reconnaissance Staffeln
Coastal "	3 Staffeln of different types.

Staffeln

4. A Staffel is a mobile operational unit which may be commanded by a Major, Captain or Lieutenant. For tactical purposes only it may be divided into two or three SCHWARME (generally 5 aircraft) or KETTEN (generally 3 aircraft).

A cutaway of the twin-engine Messerschmitt Bf 110, an aircraft that was no match for the RAF Spitfires and Hurricanes.

The *Handbook on German Military Forces* is actually a US technical manual published towards the end of the war, but it remains useful for deepening our understanding of the Luftwaffe's organisation, particularly in terms of the structures beyond that of pure combat units. In September 1939, the Luftwaffe comprised a total of 2,564 operational aircraft, divided between 302 *Staffeln*. During 1940, the volumes of German fighter aircraft production leapt from 605 units in 1939 to 2,746 in 1940, although the rise in output was necessary to meet both combat losses in Western Europe and also attrition to mechanical failure in hard-pushed machines.

From *Handbook on German Military Forces* (1945)

CHAPTER X
German Air Force

Section I. AIR FORCE HIGH COMMAND

1. General

The German Air Force (*Luftwaffe*), one of the three branches of the German Armed Forces, is organized and administered independently of either the Army or the Navy. Its three main branches are the flying troops, antiaircraft artillery, and air signal troops. It also includes parachute and airborne troops, air engineers, air medical corps, and air police, and a number of special divisions formed of Air Force personnel for service as regular fighting troops. It is organized on a territorial rather than a functional basis, with separate operational and administrative commands. This division of responsibilities has made for a high degree of mobility among the flying units and thus has been responsible for much of the success of the German Air Force.

2. Commander-in-Chief

Reichsmarschall Goering serves in the dual capacity of Minister of Aviation (*Reichsminister der Luftfahrt*) and Commander-in-Chief of the Air Force (*Oberbefehlshaber der Luftwaffe*). As Commander-in-Chief he is charged with the administration and operations of the Air Force. As Minister of Aviation he is a member of the Cabinet and is responsible for the coordination and supervision of civil aviation. Since Goering has many other duties in the German Government, however, the supreme command usually is exercised by the State Secretary in the Ministry of Aviation and Inspector General of the Air Force.

3. Air Ministry (*Reichsluftfahrtministerium* or *R.L.M.*)

At the Air Ministry – the highest administrative and operational authority of the Air Force – are found the departments which control all Air Force activity. These departments fall into two groups: those of the General Staff and those concerned with administration and supply.

Section II. CHAIN OF COMMAND

1. General

The role of the Air Force in the conduct of the war, and to a certain extent in particular operations, is determined by the High Command of the Armed Forces

(*Oberkommando der Wehrmacht*). The chain of command is from the Supreme Commander (Hitler), through the *OKW* to the Commander-in-Chief of the Air Force (Goering). The latter directs the actual employment of the Air Force through the Air Ministry and through his subordinate commanders of air combat units. However, when Air Force units are used in conjunction with Army or Navy units, all the forces involved come under a single operational control, in accordance with the German doctrine of unity of command. In such circumstances, a commanding officer is chosen from whichever of the three branches predominates in the operation, and he becomes directly responsible to the *OKW*.

2. *Luftflotte*

All Air Force units are organized into tactical and territorial air commands known as *Luftflotten*. Each *Luftflotte* is assigned a particular command area, although this assignment is not necessarily permanent, for an entire *Luftflotte* at any time may be moved from one area to another at the direction of the Air Ministry. Within its area, however, each *Luftflotte* not only controls all operations of the flying units, but also supervises the activities of all ground service units. Thus, in addition to a large operations department, each *Luftflotte* has its own adjutant, legal, administration, signal, and supply departments. All commands and formations subordinate to the *Luftflotte* are either essentially operational (*Fliegerkorps, Jagdkorps, Geschwader, Gruppen*, and *Staffeln*) or administrative (*Luftgaue*). Thus the administrative and operational commands meet at the *Luftflotte* headquarters, where their respective activities are coordinated.

3. *Fliegerkorps*

Operational units within the *Luftflotte* command area are organized into subordinate operational commands known as *Fliegerkorps*. Through these *Fliegerkorps*, the *Luftflotten* execute the operational directives received from the Air Ministry. Each *Fliegerkorps* is a composite, mobile command with its own geographical area of control and operations. A *Luftflotte* may command one or several *Fliegerkorps*, depending upon the size of the command area and the nature of operations. A *Fliegerkorps* may be detached at any time for operations in another *Luftflotte* area. The makeup of a *Fliegerkorps* is very elastic, both as to number and type of aircraft. It may consist of several bomber *Geschwader*, several fighter *Geschwader*, in addition to a varying number of short- and long-range reconnaissance *Gruppen*. On occasion it may be limited to one function such as that of a bomber command. The most important department of the *Fliegerkorps* command is that of operations. Although the *Fliegerkorps* also has adjutant, legal, administration, signal, and supply departments, it depends almost entirely upon the *Luftgau* for administrative and supply services. The *Fliegerkorps* are numbered nonconsecutively in Roman numerals.

The Heinkel He 111 was Germany's principal bomber type.

4. *Jagdkorps*

A *Jagdkorps* is an operational command, similar to a *Fliegerkorps* but whose function is limited to that of a fighter command.

5. *Fliegerdivision*

A *Fliegerdivision* is an operational command similar to but of less importance than a *Fliegerkorps*. Most of the *Fliegerdivisionen* which existed prior to the war were replaced by *Fliegerkorps*. Several *Fliegerdivisionen* still exist on the Eastern Front.

6. *Jagddivision*

A *Jagddivision* is a command subordinate to a *Jagdkorps*.

7. *Lehrdivision*

This division is unnumbered and is known simply as the *Lehrdivision*. Its primary function was to test the latest types of aircraft, antiaircraft defenses, and air signals equipment from a tactical and operational point of view. *Lehr* units are incorporated directly into the combat commands and function as a part of the command's operational strength. *Lehr* personnel are supposed to have had previous combat experience. This system, by giving the *Lehr* units an operational status, enables them to experiment in actual combat operations, rather than under simulated conditions. The *Lehrdivision* was organized into a variety of formations and commands. There were two *Lehrgeschwader* composed of bomber, fighter, and reconnaissance *Lehrgruppen*. Recently, however, only a few bomber *Lehr* units have been operational and they no longer appear concerned with experimentation. There are also two

Lehrregimenter, one concerned with antiaircraft defenses and the other with signal developments. *Lehr* units are not to be confused with experimental units whose duties are of a technical nature, such as the testing of prototype aircraft.

8. *Geschwader*

a. GENERAL. The *Geschwader* is the largest mobile, homogeneous formation in the Air Force, and is used for long-range bombers, ground attack units, and both single- and twin-engine fighters. It normally consists of about 100 aircraft, organized into three *Gruppen*. A fourth and, in a few instances, a fifth *Gruppe* have been added to several single-engine fighter *Geschwader*. Apparently the original intention was to have each *Geschwader* operate as a unit by stationing all three *Gruppen* at adjacent airdromes. However, although all *Gruppen* are now usually found on the same battlefront, all three of them are unlikely to operate from neighboring fields. In fact, it is not uncommon at present for the Air Force to withdraw one or two *Gruppen* for rest or re-equipment and subsequently return them to operations in another theater.

b. COMMAND. A *Geschwader* is generally commanded by an *Oberst* or *Oberstleutnant* known as the *Geschwaderkommodore*. He has a small Staff of officers for the adjutant, operations, organization, technical, signal, navigation, meteorological, and intelligence branches. Some staffs also have a photographic officer. The staff has its own headquarters flight (*Stabs-Schwärm*) of three to six aircraft of the same type as those which make up the *Geschwader*. This *Geschwader* staff is always maintained, even when the subordinate *Gruppen* are separated for operations on different fronts.

c. TYPES. There are several types of *Geschwader*, known according to aircraft complement and/or operational employment as follows:

German title	*Aircraft type*	*Abbreviation*
Kampfgeschwader	Bomber	*K. G.*
Schlachtgeschwader	Ground attack and antitank	*S.G.*
Jadgeschwader	Single-engine fighter	*J. G.*
Zerstorergeschwader	Twin-engine fighter	*Z. G.*
Nachtjagdgeschwader	Night fighter	*N. J. G.*
Lehrgeswader	Tactical experimental	*L. G.*

Each *Geschwader* is designated by its abbreviation followed by an Arabic numeral: for example, *K.G.77, N.J.G.26, Z.G.111*, etc. The numerals are not necessarily in consecutive order.

d. EQUIPMENT. Although all *Gruppen* in a *Geschwader* specialize in similar air tactics and are equipped with the same type of plane, the make and model may differ among the *Gruppen*. This variation is most prevalent in fighter *Geschwader*, but also occurs in a few of the bomber *Geschwader*. Thus a *Kampfgeschwader* may have one *Gruppe* equipped with the Dornier 217 and the other two *Gruppen* with the Heinkel 111, Junkers 88, or the Focke-Wulf 200. Or the entire *Geschwader* may be equipped with the same make of plane, such as the Messerschmitt 109, although one *Gruppe* may have a newer model while the other *Gruppen* have earlier ones.

9. *Gruppe*

a. GENERAL. The *Gruppe* is the basic combat unit of the Air Force for both administrative and operational purposes. It is a mobile homogeneous unit which is largely self-contained and which may be detached from its parent *Geschwader* for operations in any command area. In fact, directives for the movement of flying units are almost always issued in terms of *Gruppen*. Usually the entire *Gruppe* is based at the same airdrome.

b. COMMAND. The *Gruppe* normally is commanded by a major or captain known as the *Gruppenkommandeur*. He has a small staff, consisting of the adjutant, operations officer, technical officer, and medical officer. There apparently is no special intelligence officer, since prisoners are sent directly to interrogation centers. Each *Gruppe* also has its own air signal platoon (*Luftnachrichtenzug*), known as a Technical Ground Station, and a staff flight (*Stabs-Kette*) of three aircraft generally of the same type with which the *Gruppe* is equipped.

c. EQUIPMENT. The *Gruppen* are organized into three *Staffeln*, with the exception of single-engine fighter *Geschwadern* which recently have been organized into four *Staffeln*. Thus, most *Gruppen* are considered to have a table of organization of 27 aircraft each (exclusive of the three aircraft of the *Gruppen-Stab*) and *Jagdgruppen* a table of organization of 36 aircraft (also exclusive of the *Gruppen-Stab*). Actual strength, however, is likely to differ substantially from authorized strength; on many occasions it has been found well below or above such figures. *Gruppen* attached to a *Geschwader* are numbered in Roman numerals in consecutive order. Thus *I/K. G. 77*, *II/K. G. 77*, and *III/K. G. 77* are the first, second, and third *Gruppen*, respectively, of long-range bomber *Geschwader 77*.

10. *Staffel*

a. GENERAL. The *Staffel* is the smallest Air Force operational unit, and is generally commanded by a captain or lieutenant known as the *Staffelkapitan*. One officer serves as adjutant; the signal, technical, and navigation branches are supervised by the flying personnel in their spare time.

b. EQUIPMENT. A *Staffel* is considered to have a table of organization of nine aircraft. Its actual strength, however, may be as low as five or six aircraft or as much as 18 or 20 aircraft. For tactical purposes, it may be subdivided into *Schwarme* of five

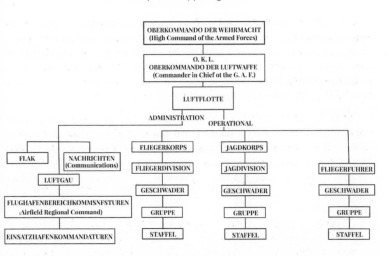

planes; into *Ketten* of three planes; or into *Rotten* of two planes. Each *Staffel* usually will have its own mobile repair shop for minor repairs in the dispersal areas; other motor vehicles must be drawn from the organization of the parent *Gruppe*.

c. NUMBERING. All *Staffeln* in the *Geschwader* are numbered consecutively in Arabic numerals.

Thus, in all but *Jagdgeschwader*, the first, second, and third *Staffeln* constitute *Gruppe I*; the fourth, fifth and sixth *Staffeln*, *Gruppe II*; and the seventh, eighth, and ninth *Staffeln*, *Gruppe III*. Where a fourth or fifth *Gruppe* exists, the *Staffeln* will be numbered 10, 11, and 12, or 13, 14, and 15, respectively. In *Jagdgeschwadern* having four *Staffeln*, the *Gruppe I* thus will contain *Staffeln* 1, 2, 3, and 4; *Gruppe II*, *Staffeln* 5, 6, 7, and 8; *Gruppe III*, *Staffeln* 9, 10, 11, and 12; etc. In unit designations, the *Gruppe* numeral is omitted whenever the *Staffel* number is indicated. Thus the fourth Staffel of *K. G. 77* is known as *4/K. G. 77*, and no other reference to its position in *Gruppe II* of *K. G. 77* is necessary.

11. Semi-autonomous Units

a. GENERAL. Reconnaissance and Army cooperation aircraft operate and are organized as semi-autonomous units, as *Staffeln* or *Gruppen*. These semi-autonomous units fall into three general categories, all of which are numbered nonconsecutively in Arabic numerals of one, two or three digits.

b. LONG-RANGE RECONNAISSANCE. Long-range reconnaissance aircraft are organized into *Fernaufklärungsgruppen*, which are known as *(F)* or *FAG* units. Thus *3(F)123* is the third *Staffel* of *Fernaufklärungsgruppe 123*.

c. SHORT-RANGE RECONNAISSANCE. Short-range reconnaissance and Army cooperation aircraft are organized into *Nahaufklärungsgruppen*, which are known as *NAGr* or *(H)* units (due to former name of *Heeresaufklärungsgruppen*). Under the old nomenclature still applying to some units, the first *Staffel* of *Nahaufklärungsgruppe 32* is therefore *1(H)32*. Under the more recent *Gruppen* organization and numbering, the third *Staffel* of *Nahaufklärungsgruppe 1* for instance, is *3/NAGr 1*.

d. COASTAL RECONNAISSANCE. Coastal reconnaissance and naval cooperation aircraft were originally organized into *Küstenfliegergruppen* (abbreviated *K.F.Gr.*). They are now known as *Seeaufklärungsgruppen* (abbreviated *SAGr.*). Thus the third *Staffel* of *Seeaufklärungsgruppe 196* is known as *3/SAGr. 196*.

e. MISCELLANEOUS UNITS. Miscellaneous units also are similarly organized and operated.

(1) *Nachtschlachtgruppen* (Night Harassing) represent the relatively recent grouping of previously loosely organized *Staffeln*. Most of them are equipped with obsolete aircraft, although coincidentally with their reorganization in *Gruppen*, these units have been modernized to some extent. Though some units in the East still have such aircraft as Arado 66, G0145, HE50, etc., those in the West are equipped with modern Ju 87 and Fw 190. These *Nachtschlachtgruppen* are numbered in Arabic numbers and thus abbreviated— *NS1, NS2, NS3*, etc.

(2) The *Luftbeobachter Staffeln* (Air Observers).

(3) A number of specialized units such as minesweeping *Staffeln*, etc.

12. Special Commands

a. *Jagdführer*. Separate fighter commands known as *Jagdführer*, or more commonly as *Jafü*, have been established in each *Luftflotte* since the outbreak of war. At first a *Jafü* was concerned primarily with matters of policy and controlled operations only on specific occasions. Yet, for a period, the *Jafüs* in France and Germany appeared to have had an overriding authority in directing all defensive fighter operations. Lately, however, it is believed that their functions have become virtually administrative.

b. *Fliegerführer*. Highly specialized operations on certain fronts have been put under the control of special commanders known as *Fliegerführer*. These *Fliegerführer* control operations in a particular area only and are directly responsible to the *Luftflottecommander* in whose area they operate. For instance, the three *Fliegerführer* (3, 4, 5) in *Luftflotte V*, although primarily concerned with anti-shipping operations and weather reconnaissance, controlled all types of combat aircraft in their area of operations.

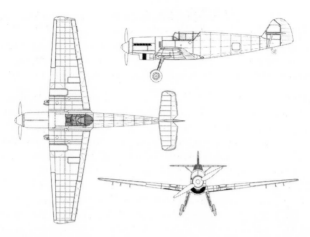

The Messerschmitt Bf 109 fighter was the Luftwaffe's most prolific fighter aircraft. (B. Huber)

13. *Luftgau*

a. GENERAL. The *Luftgaue* are the actual administrative and supply organizations of the *Luftwaffe*. They are stationary or immobile commands whose authority is limited to certain well defined and permanently fixed geographical areas. A *Luftgau* commander is usually a *General der Flieger* or *General der Flakartillerie*, and theoretically is responsible to the *Luftflotte* commander within whose command area the *Luftgau* lies. In actual practice, however, the *Luftgau* commanders receive most of their instructions direct from the Air Ministry, and the *Luftflottenchefs* interfere little with *Luftgau* administration. The *Luftgaue* permanently established in Germany are numbered non-consecutively by Roman numerals; those in occupied countries are generally designated by their location: for example, *Luftgau Norwegen*.

b. FUNCTIONS. Each *Luftgau* is responsible for the following services within its command area:

(1) Administration, supply, and maintenance of all flying units.
(2) Active and passive defense against air attack.
(3) Operations of signal units.
(4) All training other than that of auxiliary units.
(5) Recruitment, mobilization, and training of reserve personnel.

c. SECTIONS. Each *Luftgau* has its own operations, adjutant, legal, administration, signal, and supply sections. It also has a department for prohibited and restricted flying areas which has no known counterpart in the *Luftflotte* or *Fliegerkorps* headquarters. All training within the *Luftgau* area is directed by a Higher Commander of Training. This officer is usually a *Generalmajor* and is subordinate only to the *Luftgau* commander. All other *Luftgau* services are maintained through subordinate section commands which are designated by Arabic numerals preceding the *Luftgau* unit designation. Thus 4/VIII is the fourth section command in *Luftgau* VIII.

d. AIRDROME COMMANDS. The main channels through which the flying units draw on the services of the *Luftgaue* are the airdrome commands. Each *Luftgau* area is divided into about five airdrome regional commands (*Flughafenbereichkommandanturen*). The regional commands are in turn subdivided into five or more operational airdrome commands (*Einsatzhafenkommandanturen*). The regional command is essentially administrative and is not necessarily located at an airfield. The operational airdrome command, however, exists only to serve the flying units at their stations and is thus always found at an airdrome. The manner in which the *Luftgau* has decentralized its authority through these commands is as follows:

(1) The airdrome regional commands are charged with the *Luftgau's* responsibility for supply and maintenance of supplies and equipment within their respective areas; meeting the physical needs of the flying units; defense of aircraft, equipment, and motor transport against air attack; airdrome development; and air movements. These duties are discharged by specialized units which the *Luftgau* allots to the regional command and which the regional command then redistributes among the operational commands. For example, the Field Works Office (*Feldbauamt*) at the regional command handles airdrome maintenance through its subsidiary Works Superintendent's Offices which are stationed at the airdromes. Similarly, the Air Signal Company at each regional command is divided into platoons which are stationed at the operational commands. A senior technical officer supervises aircraft maintenance in the region through his subordinate technical officers at the operational commands. The airdrome regional command is thus largely self-contained and calls on the *Luftgau* for assistance only when the units already assigned prove inadequate.

(2) The airdrome regional command also acts as the intermediary between the *Luftgau* headquarters and the operational airdrome command. All orders, requests, reports, etc., traveling between the two must pass through the regional command staff. This staff numbers from 50 to 150 officers and enlisted men and is headed by a commandant who usually holds the rank of *General-major*.

(3) The airdrome regional command's primary practical task is that of transporting supplies and equipment from the depots to its subordinate operational commands. For this purpose it is generally assigned a supply company (*Nachschubkompanie*) composed of a supply column staff (*Nachschubkolonnenstab*),

some four transport columns (*Transportkolonnen*), and two or three fuel-columns (*Flugbetriebsstoffkolonnen*).

(4) The commander of the operational airdrome command normally holds the rank of major, captain, or first lieutenant. His adjutant handles personnel matters. The personnel complement of an operational command numbers about 350 officers and enlisted men, and the motor transport allotment is between 50 and 100 vehicles.

(5) Airdrome maintenance at each operational command is handled by a Works Superintendent's Office (*Bauleitung*), subordinate to the Field Works Office at the regional command. The *Bauleitung* has charge of most of the construction done at the airdrome (buildings, dispersal areas, defense works, camouflage, etc.), as well as the laying of runways, extension of landing grounds, and installation of lighting systems. Reports on serviceability and bomb damage are radioed through the regional command to the *Luftgau*, and thence to the Air Ministry for broadcast over the Air Force Safety Service network. The *Bauleitung* personnel is composed of civil servants and technical staffs. Any other specialized construction units which may be attached to the airdromes to repair bomb damage or enlarge facilities are also directed by the *Bauleitung*.

(6) The operational airdrome command is also responsible for defense against air attack, for which it has both heavy and light *Flak* units. These guns and other aerial defense units are commanded by the airdrome commander only when there is no flying unit stationed at the field. Otherwise, defense is controlled by the commander of that flying unit which is occupying the airdrome.

(7) The telephone, teleprinter, and radio at each operational airdrome command are operated by an air signal platoon (*Fliegerhorst-Luftnachrichtenzug*) and commanded by a signal officer who is subordinate to the senior signal officer at the airdrome regional command. The signal platoon also transmits the meteorological and airdrome serviceability reports and operates the Air Movements Control. This control directs only non-operational flying. Signal communications with aircraft in operations are controlled by the tactical ground station attached to the flying unit.

(8) Aircraft maintenance at the operational airdrome command—except for servicing and minor repairs which are performed by the ground staff of the flying unit—is the responsibility of a technical officer. This officer not only handles overhauls and major repairs, but also is responsible for maintenance of motor vehicles; for bomb, fuel, and other supply stores; and for equipment stores and the armory. He is subordinate to the senior technical officer at the airdrome regional command.

(9) The requests by the operational airdrome command for equipment and spare parts reach the regional command through the technical officer. Requisitions for

bombs, fuel, and ammunition are made by the supply section. The operational command also has an administrative section which handles clothing, food, pay, billeting, and other accommodations; a record office; a photographic section; a medical section; and a welfare section.

(10) *Luftgaustäbe z.b.V.* During campaigns the *Luftgaue* provide the advancing air formation with supplies and services through a system of subordinate commands known as *Luftgaustäbe zur besonderer Verwendung* (*Luftgau* staffs for special duty) or, simply, *Luftgaustäbe z.b.V.* units. These units may be designated by an Arabic numeral (*Luftgaustab z.b.V. 3*) or by their location (*Luftgaustab Kiev*). They are sent into the forward battle areas by their controlling *Luftgau* and are normally responsible for all services in an area occupied by a *Fliegerkorps*. After conditions have become relatively stabilized—for example, when operational airdrome commands have been established and supply stations and fuel and ammunition field depots have been set up—the *Luftgaustäb z.b.V.* unit is withdrawn and the parent *Luftgau* assumes direct command.

Section III. AIR FORCE ARMS AND SERVICES

I. Antiaircraft Defenses

a. GENERAL. The bulk of the German antiaircraft artillery, inclusive of antiaircraft searchlight units, is an organic part of the German Air Force. The German Army has antiaircraft artillery units of its own, but these units are only for the organic use and protection of the Army units against air attack.

[. . .]

b. ANTIAIRCRAFT DEFENSE OF GERMANY AND REAR AREAS. The Chief of the German Air Force is responsible for the air defense of territorial Germany as well as important installations in occupied countries. The Aircraft Warning Service as a part of the Air Force is tied in with the coordinated use of aviation, antiaircraft artillery, and barrage balloons. All air raid precaution measures also are the responsibility of the Chief of the German Air Force.

Antiaircraft defense of rear areas is carried out through the *Luftgaue* mentioned above. *Luftgaue* coordinate their defenses with each other in accordance with regulations published by the Chief of the Air Force. The commander of each *Luftgau* has a specialist under him who exercises command over the antiaircraft artillery units, including searchlights, assigned to the district. Other specialists include the commanders of barrage balloon units and of units responsible for carrying out special defense measures. In actual operations, in most cases the commands above the actual operating units act mainly in a coordinating capacity, feeding information to the operating units which act in turn on their own initiative in accordance with prescribed standing operating procedure.

Within certain of the air districts there are special air defense commands. Each of these covers special areas or cities of vital importance, defense of which, under one command, is laid out with a concentration of coordinated defense facilities inclusive of antiaircraft guns and searchlights, fighter aviation, barrage balloons, warning facilities, and the use of special devices such as smoke generators.

Operation of the antiaircraft defense system calls for close cooperation between fighter planes and air warning systems, and the antiaircraft guns with supporting searchlights are considered the backbone of the static defense. For operational control, the antiaircraft command in a *Luftgau* is usually divided into groups known as *Flakgruppen*, and these groups in turn are divided into sub-groups known as *Flakuntergruppen*. The headquarters of the group is normally the control center of the *Flak* defenses, and acts downward through the sub-groups.

In deployment of heavy antiaircraft guns in important static areas, there is a tendency toward the use of concentrated sites known as *Grossbatterien*. These usually consist of three 4-, 6-, or even 8-gun batteries grouped together at one site, with fire control for all guns emanating from one central source.

Antiaircraft searchlights are used in cooperation with night fighters, as well as in their normal role of illuminating targets for the gun units.

[. . .]

The Junkers Ju 87 dive-bomber.

2. German Air Force Signal Service (*Luftnachrichtenwesen*)

a. GENERAL. The importance of a comprehensive and efficient air signal service in aerial warfare is obvious. Neither offensive nor defensive air operations could be conducted without a complete network of signal communications, or without radio and radar equipment for the direction and control of aircraft, particularly in fighter defense. So vital is the role of the German Air Force Signal Service that it has had a greater proportionate wartime expansion than any other arm of the German Air Force, and now has an estimated personnel strength of between 175,000 and 200,000.

b. FLEXIBILITY. The efficiency of the German Air Force has been enhanced by the flexibility of its signal organization. This was particularly true when the Germans were advancing into new territory, usually well prepared, on a temporary basis, for the reception of flying units. As soon as the captured territory was firmly occupied, signal units then established a more permanent land-line communications system. Under present circumstances, with the Germans on the defensive, the flexibility and mobility of the German Air Force are no longer dependent to the same extent on its signal organization. However, a workable German Air Force Signal Service is still of paramount importance in the defense of Germany against air attacks.

c. FUNCTIONS. These include the transmission of all orders and communications necessary for the operation and functioning of the German Air Force, if possible both by land-line and by wireless; the establishment and supervision of all navigational aids to aircraft; the manning of Observer Corps and radar in connection with air defense; control of air traffic, air safety and rescue services; and the interception of enemy signals.

d. ORGANIZATION. (1) *General.* One of the departments of the German Air Ministry is the Director General of Signal Communications (*Generalnachrichtenführer der Luftwaffe*). To handle its multiple duties, a flexible organization has been developed, consisting of many self-contained specialist companies. The bulk of these companies are allocated to the major operational and administrative commands, and the others are grouped into battalions or remain as individual companies attached to minor commands.

(2) *Section platoon and company.* The basic operational unit is the section (*Truppe*) of 10–20 men. Each section specializes in one particular signal activity such as telephone, teletype, cable laying, construction, etc. Five to ten sections of the same type are organized into a platoon (*Zug*) of 80 to 100 men. Three to six platoons are grouped into a company (*Kompanie*) of 200 to 300 men. All platoons in a company specialize in the same branch of signal activity, so that each company is a self-contained specialist unit.

(3) *Battalion and regiment.* Three to four companies usually make up a battalion (*Abteilung*), although some have many more. The strength of a battalion, aside from its staff, depends on the number of companies. Three to five battalions normally form a regiment (*Regimenter*), with a strength between 1,500 and 9,000 and varying functions.

(4) *Allotment and numbering of units.* Signal regiments and smaller units are allotted to the several different types of operational and administrative commands requiring a permanent allocation of signal personnel. Allocation is on the basis of the size and requirements of the command. The relationship of the signal units to their assigned commands often is indicated by the terminal number of the unit designation; e.g. *Luftflotte 2* had Signal Regiments 2, 12, and 22. However, with the creation of many new commands and the renumbering of others, the numbering system for signal units is not as readily workable as formerly.

(5) *Special units.* In addition to the standard units, there is a special Research Regiment charged with the development of new types of signal equipment and its employment. Aircraft specially equipped for signal activities have also in many instances been allotted to various commands and have proved extremely useful in conducting air operations in mobile situations.

(6) *Command.* The supreme signal command of the above units is exercised by the Director General of Signals of the Air Ministry. Signal command of a *Luftflotte* is under a Chief Signal Officer (*Hohere Nachrichtenführer* or *Hohere Nafü*) who controls the senior Signal Officer (*Nafü*) of the *Fliegerkorps, Luftgaue, Flak-Korps* and *Flak Division*, and Airfield Regional Command. Subordinate to these are the Signal Officers (*Nachrichten Offizieror N. O.*) who exercise command in the lower subdivisions such as Operational Airfield Command signal platoons, and *Geschwader* signal companies.

e. SIGNAL EQUIPMENT. (1) *General.* German signal equipment, generally speaking, has been characterized by standardization of design, relatively few major types, and a high quality of components and workmanship. During the first years of the war, the Germans did not fully appreciate the tactical possibilities of radar and for a time Allied radar development was well ahead of the German. However, the Germans have made tremendous efforts to match Allied technical progress and to overcome the various tactical problems resulting from Allied superiority.

(2) *Ground radar.* German ground radar falls into three general categories: Early warning set (*Freya, Mammutor* or *Wassermann*) for long range detection; *Giant Würzburg* primarily for aircraft interception control; and *Small Würzburg* designed for flak control, but also used for height finding in the Aircraft Reporting Service. These various types of ground radar equipment play a large part in the German

system of air raid warning and control of fighter interception. Many devices have been developed by the Allies to nullify the effectiveness of the German equipment, but at the same time the Germans have developed numerous counter-measures. These measures and counter-measures have led to extremely rapid development of new techniques and equipment both by the Germans and by the Allies.

(3) *Airborne radio and radar.* German airborne radio and radar equipment may be classified in four general categories: *Funkgerat (FuG)*, or radio and radar equipment involving transmitters and receivers; *Peilgerat (PeG)*, or navigational equipment; *Notsender (NS)*, or emergency transmitter; and other types of miscellaneous equipment. Airborne equipment is an absolute necessity for the successful conduct of air operations. Throughout the war, the Germans have developed navigational, bombing, and fighter control equipment. The latter is particularly important at the present time for the Germans who must depend on adequate warning of Allied air attacks and efficient control of fighters and flak for effective opposition.

f. FIGHTER DEFENSE. (1) *General.* During 1941 and early 1942, the German Air Force fighter organization was concerned mainly with defense of targets in Northern France and the Lowlands. The bulk of aerial combats then were taking place in the relatively small area over those countries and over the English Channel; and a warning system, consisting of a coastal radar belt and visual observers, was adequate. But the greater depth of penetration by Allied bombers in 1943 required that the German Air Force protect targets in Germany as well as in occupied territory, and the defensive problem thus became infinitely more complex. Additional radar belts and observer posts were required. German fighters had to be placed in tactically favorable positions, and they were forced to enlarge the scope of their activity to cover all areas subject to attack. Such developments naturally led to considerable changes in the German Air Force fighter organization and the methods of fighter control. The liberation of France and part of the Lowlands in 1944 further complicated the German defensive problem by depriving the German Air Force of a large and efficient part of its early warning system, as well as many excellent airfields at a time when the weight of the Allied air assault was increasing.

(2) *Reporting and warning system.* The Aircraft Reporting Service is a part of the German Air Force. Long-range radar sets determine the range and bearing of the approaching aircraft, and short-range sets measure height. Other types of equipment distinguish between friendly and hostile aircraft. An Observer Corps network with strategically located posts also supplies aircraft warning information, while in some instances patrolling aircraft shadow the attacking aircraft. On the basis of the information from these various sources, hostile aircraft are plotted in a central headquarters, and the Germans in the past have been able to construct a fairly accurate and current picture of Allied air operations. Proper warning then is given to all interested agencies, and defensive fighters are put in the air to intercept the

attackers. Information on the course and expected target of the bombers is passed by radio to the airborne fighters until contact is made. The specific aerial tactics used by the German fighters have varied considerably throughout the war, but in general the precise method becomes the responsibility of the fighter pilots after contact is made. In spite of the excellent equipment and control methods the Germans have developed, their defensive warnings and operations are considerably handicapped by the loss of territory in Western Europe.

CHAPTER 2

THE DEFENCE OF
GREAT BRITAIN

In many ways, Britain was ill-prepared to defend itself against a determined enemy air campaign when the war began in 1939. Until 1936, the overarching British organisation dedicated to the matter of aerial warfare was the Air Defence of Great Britain (ADGB). The ADGB was an unwieldly umbrella structure, and in 1936 it was split up into a number of separate commands, each defined by its primary role: Fighter, Bomber, Coastal, Reserve and Training. (Notably, Fighter Command also had control over the Army's Anti-Aircraft Command, when it came to matters of defending the British mainland.) In practical terms, this meant that Fighter Command was still a relatively new entity by the time it faced the Battle of Britain in 1940. It fell upon Dowding to create, in haste, an integrated and quick-reacting fighter force, incorporating the latest fighters (Hurricanes and Spitfires only reached frontline service in significant numbers in 1939) and also the critical technology of air defence radar. This he accomplished through the 'Dowding System', a regional network of air defence that took information from radar detection and Observer Corps sightings and filtered it rapidly down through Command, Group and Sector operations rooms. It mostly worked well, and came just at the point in history when Britain needed a smooth-running human and technical response to an immediate threat.

In the first of our sources, the *Royal Air Force War Manual* considers the key principles of fighting an air war. Note also that this includes aspects of anti-aircraft artillery defence; the thump of AA guns would be just as much a signature of the Battle of Britain as the drone of aircraft engines.

From *Royal Air Force War Manual, Part 1, Operations*, 2nd edition
(February 1940)

CHAPTER IV THE PRINCIPLES AND CONDUCT OF AIR WARFARE

General Considerations

1. Commonsense and a balanced judgment are qualities indispensable to the successful commander in air warfare. These two qualities are just as essential to the commander in war as they are to the ordinary citizen in the conduct of his business or his profession in everyday life; but the conditions of war are very different from those of everyday life; the time factor is more urgent, information is harder to get and less reliable, and the elements of danger and fatigue are more often present; despite the greatest amount of forethought the unforeseen frequently occurs and casualties upset preconceived plans.

2. In order to meet these unfamiliar and exacting conditions, the commander's commonsense and judgment must be backed by a sound knowledge of certain basic precepts which have marked the successes of commanders in past wars. These basic precepts or "principles" are not laws, such as the laws of natural science where the observance of certain conditions produces an inevitable result, nor yet rules, such as the rules of a game, the breach of which entails a definite penalty; they simply indicate methods of action that have proved successful in the past, and they serve as a warning that their disregard involves risk and has often brought failure.

3. In any air operation, great or small, it is the duty of the commander to define clearly to himself the aim which he is seeking to attain and thereafter to *maintain that aim*, allowing nothing to distract him from it. He should then apply to his task the commonsense rules which have guided all fighting since the earliest days. First, he must realize that *offensive action* alone will bring success in air warfare as in any other kind of warfare; he must also try to surprise and distract the enemy, since an enemy thrown off his guard is at a serious moral and physical disadvantage. The commander must *concentrate* his whole effort, moral, physical and material, upon achieving the purpose for which he is fighting and he must ensure that his concentration of effort is directed against his enemy at the critical time and place. He must see to it that there exists adequate *co-operation* and co-ordination between the various elements of his own forces and with any other force with which he is working. It is commonsense, too, that he should exercise *economy in the use of his forces*, using the minimum for warding off his opponent's attacks or for distracting his opponent's attention and thus leaving the maximum available for attacking the enemy. Again, he must ensure that reasonable security is assured to the bases from which he is operating and to any other bases or centres whose protection is entrusted

to him. Lastly, by making use of the *mobility* of his forces he will be able to deliver his attacks at those places where they will be most effective.

4. The principles, then, that must guide the conduct of air warfare are these—

Maintenance of the Aim	Co-operation.
Offensive Action.	Economy of Force.
Surprise.	Security.
Concentration.	Mobility.

5. These are principles or maxims, in exactly the same sense that "Honesty is the best policy" and "Cut your coat according to your cloth" are maxims for the conduct of everyday life. These principles are easy enough to learn and to grasp, but they are no more a complete set of rules for success in air warfare than are the two maxims just quoted a complete guide to the conduct of everyday life. Sometimes even they are divergent in that one can only be fully observed at the expense of another. It follows then that a knowledge of these principles must be blended with the fundamental qualities of commonsense and balanced judgment which are equally essential for success in air warfare. Some further explanation of these principles of war is given below.

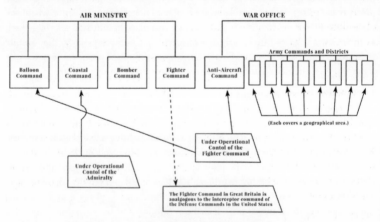

The Air Defence of Great Britain (ADGB) command structure.

The Principles of Air Warfare

6. *Maintenance of the Aim.*—To every commander, from an Air Officer Commanding-in-Chief down to the pilot of an individual aircraft, an aim should be given for the operation immediately in hand. This aim must be kept constantly in view and the commander must subordinate all his actions to its attainment.

7. In every instance the selection of a correct aim demands knowledge and judgment. The aim must be within the means of a force that can be made available to secure it, and must be that best calculated to further the favourable conclusion of the operation. When once the aim has been decided upon, all efforts must be continually directed towards its attainment so long as it is possible, and every plan of action must be tested by its bearing upon this end.

8. Diversions from the main aim are seldom justified and then only when their successful result is likely to react favourably on the attainment of the main aim; A diversion is only likely to be successful when the effort used is less than that needed by the enemy to counter it.

9. *Offensive action.*—Victory can only be won as the result of offensive action. By taking the offensive from the outset and by maintaining it with determination even in the face of reverses a commander will retain the initiative and will force his enemy on to the defensive.

10. *Surprise.*—Surprise is the most effective and powerful asset in war. With its aid a moral and material effect can be achieved out of all proportion to the amount of effort expended on it. By means of surprise an enemy, in all other respects superior, can be defeated or outwitted. The effect of surprise may be said to be proportionate to the time it takes the enemy to effect counter measures. Air warfare provides a wide scope for exploiting surprise.

11. In peace, surprise may be obtained by the development of organization; by the development of a new weapon, or of a new means of using older weapons; by the intensive preparation of a national industry for the production of war material; or by the unexpected rapidity of mobilization. In war, surprise may be gained by secrecy, by calculated stratagem devised to mislead and mystify the enemy, by unexpected rapidity of movement, or by action at an unsuspected place. Surprise loses much of its value if means are not available to make full use of its effect, as for example a surprise attack made with insufficient forces to ensure a successful issue, or a new, weapon prematurely disclosed before sufficient tests have been made or sufficient numbers are available.

12. A commander should always seek opportunities of achieving surprise and outwitting the enemy. Originality of ideas, superiority of organization, superiority of technical development and, above all, secrecy in planning are the chief means of achieving surprise.

13. *Concentration.*—The principle of concentration implies the application of moral and material pressure at the critical time and place towards the achievement of a single aim. Having decided upon that aim, a commander should concentrate upon

it his maximum effort, moral, physical and material, until such time as the results desired have been obtained.

14. *Co-operation.*—In its application to air warfare, co-operation implies the co-ordination of the various elements of air forces, such as bombing, fighting and coast defence units, to the furtherance of the role allotted to the Air Force.

15. Co-operation, both general and close, is also required between the Air Force and the sister Services during the planning stage and during the execution of the plan. Moreover, from the moral aspect the co-operation of all ranks in the common effort must be ensured by good leadership and by infusing a spirit of goodwill amongst the whole personnel.

16. *Economy of Force.*—By economy of force is meant the avoidance of wasted effort in the distribution and employment of the forces available. In most forms of air warfare a compromise must be reached between the conflicting demands of the principles of "offensive action" and "security"; but as defensive measures cannot by themselves be decisive, only the minimum compatible with reasonable security should be diverted to the defence. Similarly, when circumstances justify a diversion from the main aim, no larger force should be employed on it than is absolutely necessary.

17. Economy in the strength of air forces used for a given purpose can often be effected by taking advantage of their power of surprise and of their flexibility.

18. *Security.*—Reasonable security is the essential basis of any plan of campaign. The vital and vulnerable points in the organization of the nation must be provided with adequate protection; moreover, although only offensive action can be decisive, the bases from which the offensive is launched must be made reasonably secure.

19. This principle however, must not be held to justify undue caution and avoidance of all risks; bold action is essential to success in air warfare and security can often best be obtained by bold offensive action against the enemy.

20. *Mobility.*—Mobility in relation to air warfare implies not only the ability of aircraft to move rapidly within their range of action, but also the power of units to move quickly from one place to another and to function efficiently from their new base with the minimum of delay. The more the mobility of air force units can be increased by improvements in organization and by the provision of additional bases from which they can operate, the more readily will it be possible to concentrate air forces at the critical time and place, and thus to observe the principles of concentration and economy of force. The elements of mobility are good organization, good training, and good staff work.

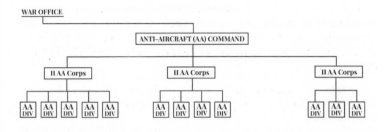

The Anti-Aircraft Command organizational structure.

CHAPTER VI
PROTECTION OF AIR FORCES WHEN ON THE GROUND

General Considerations

1. The greater freedom from hostile attack that can be provided for air forces, the more efficient will be their work in the air. In a war against an enemy employing air forces, the majority of our air stations will probably be liable to air attack, and our more forward landing grounds may, in addition, be susceptible to actual capture by the mobile surface forces of the enemy. Protection of air forces on the ground may, therefore, have to be of two kinds, namely:–

    (i) Protection against air attack.
    (ii) Protection against land attack.

Protection of Air Forces on the Ground against Air Attack

2. Active air defence is of two kinds – the *general defence* of an area by a co-ordinated system of defensive aircraft, balloons, A.A. guns, searchlights, and an aircraft wanting organization, and the *local defence* of a particular unit or site. The available A.A. artillery is not likely to be sufficient to afford individual protection to each and every air station. Therefore, air stations, whether in home territory or overseas, must rely for their main protection against high altitude bombing upon the general air defence scheme of the whole area in which they are situated.

3. Local protection against low flying attack is the responsibility of the local air force commander, whose task is to select the position and arrange for the manning of as many A.A. machine-gun and look-out posts as the size of his command demands. As the essence of effective air defence is rapidity of action in a raid, it is necessary to establish an adequate local raid warning system.

4. Every commander is also responsible for the passive defence of his command. The increased speed of aircraft tends to widen the attackers' scope for achieving surprise. The greater the surprise the less chance is there of the active defences being effective and, therefore, the greater the need for passive defences to mitigate the effects of air attack.

5. From the strategical aspect, the most effective form of passive defence is as wide a dispersal of air stations as operational requirements and the nature of the terrain will allow.

6. From the local aspect, passive defence measures should include:—

   (i) The staggering of hangars in relation to one another.
  (ii) The dispersal of aircraft picketed in the open as far as is consistent with efficiency.
 (iii) The camouflage and splinter-proofing of buildings and hutments.
 (iv) The use of any natural cover, such as woods, to conceal the presence of hangars or hutments.
  (v) The use of satellite landing grounds, if these are available, to avoid congestion on the main aerodrome.
 (vi) Lighting restriction at night.
 (vii) Precautionary measures against fire.
(viii) Raid-warning system.
 (ix) Segregation of personnel accommodation away from technical buildings as far as is consistent with efficiency.
  (x) The provision of dug-outs and shelter trenches.
 (xi) Anti-gas defence scheme.

7. All schemes for local air defence involving both active and passive measures will require the rapid manning of posts and the use of shelter. Personnel must, therefore, be constantly practised in taking their allotted raid action, and frequent practice alarms must be held.

Protection of Air Forces on the Ground against Land Attack

8. Air stations situated well forward in the vicinity of the fighting troops are liable to hostile land attack, particularly under conditions of open warfare, when the greatest threat is from enemy armoured fighting vehicles. Such aerodromes and landing grounds enjoy the general cover afforded by the fighting troops but, in addition, the air force commander is responsible for the perimeter defence of his command against surprise land attack, the danger of which is greatest at night. Perimeter defence measures include tank obstacles, wire entanglements, machine-gun posts, sand-bag defences and the concentration of buildings and personnel into as small an area as possible. The last of these requirements, however, runs counter to that of passive defence against air attack.

Concentration should, therefore, only be resorted to when hostile land attack alone is to be expected, as, for example, in operations against an enemy not employing air forces. When both forms of attack are to be expected, preference should be given to the requirements of defence against air attack.

9. *Sabotage.*—In operations to subdue civil disorders and, to a lesser degree, in wars against another State the danger of sabotage is always present. Sabotage may occur in a variety of forms and no fixed principles can be laid down to govern the adoption of preventive measures.

10. When, however, the possibility of sabotage is thought to exist, the precautions taken against it should include the following:—

(i) The movements of all civil or quasi-military personnel employed at or in the vicinity of air stations should be strictly supervised.
(ii) The political antecedents and police record (if any) of all civil or quasi-military personnel employed should be scrutinized, with the aid of the civil police.
(iii) Day and night pickets or patrols should be organized in the vicinity of aircraft and other important material.

[. . .]

CHAPTER IX
THE STRATEGIC AIR DEFENSIVE

General Considerations

1. The defensive role of the Air Force is to provide defence against air attack. The *ultimate* result which may be expected to accrue from a strong air offensive will in due course contribute towards the defence of our territory against air attack; but air offensive measures will not afford *immediate* protection from the enemy's air attacks upon our territory.

2. Therefore other steps must be taken to achieve the maximum defence practicable against air attack. It is with these other measures, which are strategically defensive in character, that this chapter is concerned.

Defensive Strategy

3. By reason of the evasive powers of aircraft, no form of protection against air attack can be absolute. However strong our air defence may be, some of the enemy air forces will succeed in penetrating it and in delivering their bombs. Nevertheless by opposing the enemy's raiding forces with vigour and determination it will be possible steadily to diminish the effectiveness of his air offensive. Our purpose must be to cause heavy casualties amongst the enemy's

raiding forces, and thus convince him that further raids in that area are no longer profitable.

4. In a war against a first-class power it will not be possible to intercept every raid that attacks our territory; it should therefore be our aim to concentrate on particular raids that have been, or can be, intercepted and to endeavour to destroy them completely. The moral effect on the enemy of the complete destruction of one raid will be greater than that of small toll taken of a number of raids. It is preferable that raids should be attacked before they have reached their objective.

5. It is probable that the enemy, when planning his attacks, will endeavour to force us to split up our defensive forces into small components, too weak to be effective. We must resist a tendency to dissipate the strength of our defence.

The Constitution of a Force for Air Defence

6. *The time factor.*—The vital factor in air defence is time. Aircraft travel so quickly towards their objective that probably only a short time will elapse between the entry of enemy raiding aircraft into a defended area and their arrival over their objective. It is in this short space of time that the enemy raiding aircraft must be located, engaged and destroyed.

7. *The components for air defence.*—In order to cause the maximum casualties to hostile aircraft, an air defence force must be so organized that the presence of enemy raiders approaching a defended area can be made known instantly and that rapid use can be made of this information by defensive aircraft and antiaircraft artillery. This air defence force must be capable of functioning by night as well as by day and will, whenever possible, consist of the following components working together in the closest co-operation, and adequately co-ordinated under one command:-

   (i) A force of fighter aircraft.
  (ii) Anti-aircraft artillery.
 (iii) An aircraft warning organization.
 (iv) Searchlights.
  (v) Balloon barrages.
 (vi) An intercommunication system.

8. (i) A *force of fighter aircraft.*—It is the task of this force, assisted by information from the aircraft warning organization, to find and destroy enemy raiding aircraft. At night this force depends largely upon the co-operation of searchlights for the location and illumination of hostile aircraft.

(ii) *Anti-aircraft artillery.*—Anti-aircraft artillery assists and supplements the defensive force of fighters in the destruction of enemy aircraft. At night anti-aircraft artillery fire is assisted by searchlights.

(iii) *An aircraft warning organization.*—An aircraft warning organization is composed of ground observation posts, and other devices for detecting the approach or presence of aircraft. Its task is to detect the approach of enemy raids, to estimate their height, composition and direction, and through the agency of a central control to make that information immediately available to such units of the fighter force or anti-aircraft artillery as it may concern. An organization suitably disposed throughout the defended area will help to provide not only early warning of the approach of a raid into the defended area, but also a means of keeping a track of raids.

(iv) *Searchlights.*—The purpose of searchlights, working in conjunction with sound locators, is to locate and illuminate hostile aircraft for fighters or as targets for anti-aircraft artillery.

(v) *Balloon barrages.*—Balloon barrages are designed to limit the minimum height at which hostile aircraft can operate over the defended area and thereby to simplify the task of our anti-aircraft artillery and defending aircraft.

(vi) *Intercommunication.*—For the purpose of linking all these components of the air defence system, there must be an efficient, reliable and rapid system of communication, so devised that information and instructions can be passed instantly between the various components.

9. *Degrees of air defence preparedness.*—An air defence system as described in the foregoing paragraph does not lend itself to improvisation. The degree to which the fixed or semi-fixed parts of the system can be installed before the system is put to the test of war will largely determine its effectiveness in operation.

10. In areas of British territory containing points of great strategical or national importance, it is possible to prepare an air defence system in peace time, to adjust it from time to time in the light of technical development and to test its practical efficiency by means of exercises.

11. Such comprehensive preparations, however, may not be practicable in respect of overseas areas of operations, the exact location of which we may not know in advance. Moreover, in such an area it may not be possible, for operational or topographical reasons, to provide an aircraft warning organization and other means of defence on so large a scale as is practicable for the defence of Great Britain.

12. *Active and passive defence measures.*—An active air defence system, though affording a general protection against air attack over a wide area, cannot provide equally strong local active defences to all districts in that area. Preference is therefore given to those areas containing the greatest number of objectives of vital importance. Districts of less importance must rely on passive defence measures for their local protection. Passive defence measures can do much to mitigate the effects of such raids as have penetrated the active defences.

The Strategic Employment of Fighters

13. The primary role of all fighter aircraft is the attack and destruction of enemy aircraft. The manner in which fighter aircraft can best be strategically employed as part of the air defences of a particular area will depend on what other means of air defence are available in the same area. Some of the more important methods of employing fighters as part of an air defence scheme are referred to in the following paragraphs.

14. *Interception from the ground.*—When "interception from the ground" is used, the fighters are held in readiness on the ground and are only sent up to engage the enemy when information is received of the approach of an enemy raid. This method, being dependent on the existence of a ground warning organization to detect the approach of enemy aircraft, can only be used in areas in rear of the close range zone of the enemy bombers.

15. Whenever possible this method should be used, as it is both economical and effective. Fighter aircraft can take off with full endurance to engage an enemy whose approximate location and path are known; moreover the strength of aircraft sent up can be suited to the requirements of the particular situation.

16. On the other hand, this method depends for its full effectiveness on the ability of our fighters to intercept the enemy before he reaches his objectives. The factors which govern the ability of our fighters to do so are:—

(i) The speed and height of the enemy bombers.
(ii) The rate of climb and climbing speed of our fighters.
(iii) The distance to which our warning organization is effective.
(iv) The distance over our territory that the enemy bombers have to penetrate in order to reach their objectives.

17. *Standing patrols.*—In this method of employing fighters, patrols covering a particular area are kept continuously in the air by means of successive reliefs. The patrols are maintained at a height judged to give the best chance of tactical advantage. This system may be used either with or without a warning organization to detect and report the approach of enemy aircraft. In neither case is it as economical or effective as the interception from the ground system, but when used in conjunction with a ground warning organization it is more likely to be successful than when used without such assistance.

18. *Standing patrols in conjunction with a ground warning organization.*— Standing patrols may sometimes have to be resorted to, even if a ground warning organization is available. It may be that the forward range of the warning organization is such that it cannot give sufficient warning for fighters to climb from the ground and intercept the enemy aircraft. This will arise in the defence of vulnerable points

situated in a country's close range zone near its coast line or frontier. For the air defence of such points it will be necessary to keep standing patrols in the air at high altitudes and to direct them, from the ground, to the probable point of interception, on the strength of information provided by the ground warning organization.

19. This method of employing fighters is uneconomical and likely to be less effective than the interception from the ground method. It will be found to be fatiguing for pilots who may have to spend long periods in the air at great heights and possibly without even sighting the enemy. It is extravagant in the use of aircraft, inasmuch as patrols must be of sufficient strength to deal with the largest force of enemy bombers that is likely to be encountered in that area; moreover, because of the vast three-dimensional zone which has to be guarded, a patrol can only be effective over a very limited area.

20. *Standing patrols working without the assistance of a ground warning organization.*—This method of employing fighters may have to be resorted to as being the only practicable means of affording protection to an area where no ground warning organization is available. Such a defensive system has all the disadvantages inherent in the standing patrol system mentioned in paras. 18-19 above and with the additional weakness that it depends entirely for its success on the ability of the fighter personnel in the air to search for and find an enemy approaching from a direction and at a height which to them is unknown.

[. . .]

Effective command-and-control in the RAF was imperative for governing both the daily running of the arm and also the support and implementation of fighter operations, as the first sentence of the passage below illustrates. In terms of Fighter Command missions, the most important node in the Dowding System was the Filter Room at HQ Fighter Command in RAF Bentley Priory near Stanmore, London. It was to here that all the information about incoming raids, including the data from radar and Observer Corps posts, flowed in one great mass, and where it was then processed, refined and took shape into what would become the mission orders for frontline squadrons. Those who worked in frenetic environments of the Filter Room and all the Operations Rooms needed to be of unflappable character and quick intelligence.

The text below also includes a passage relating to intelligence operations. Although radar was by far the greatest asset to detecting raids, the RAF also gleaned as much useful information as possible from intelligence reports, especially in terms of enemy units confronting it across the Channel. While some of this intelligence came from personal sources in the occupied territories, most of it came from intercepts of German radio traffic. Early on in the war, RAF Intelligence purchased several radio sets capable of listening in to German voice transmissions in mainland Europe. The radio operators gleaned much valuable information about German air strength, unit movements and intentions in this way, although it could be a struggle to find the right numbers of German speakers.

From *Royal Air Force War Manual, Part 2, Administration,*
2nd edition (1940)

CHAPTER I
Section II—The Control of the Organization

General

1. However sound the structure of an organization may be, it will not operate efficiently unless it has an efficient system of control. When the organization has to operate with the speed and certainty required to meet the war responsibilities of an air force, it is essential to provide a system of control that is quick, sensitive and smooth in operation. It is also essential to ensure that all who are responsible for the operation of the control understand its mechanism and use it to its best advantage.

2. The system of control adopted for the Royal Air Force has been built up as a result of experience and, since its inception, has undergone various modifications. It must not, therefore, be regarded as having reached finality, and it must with certain limitations always remain flexible so as to be adaptable to meet the requirements of the time.

Operations Room personnel plot the course of an enemy raid.

Two Categories of Control

3. The control of an air force falls into two broad but interrelated categories, operational control and administrative control. Operational control is concerned with the direction of the activities of the fighting units, whilst administrative control is concerned with marshalling all the resources available to a fighting service so that the fighting units can achieve their maximum operational efficiency.

4. It is a fundamental principle that operational control must not be hindered by administrative detail, and that administrative control must work in accordance with operational requirements. Thus, though in many instances administrative control may be separated from operational control the two must at all time be correlated to ensure that administrative arrangements are keeping pace with operational requirements or what is equally important, to ensure that operations are not being planned on a scale beyond the administrative capacity of the units having regard to the resources available to them.

Operational Control—Home Commands

5. The general policy regarding the operational employment of the Royal Air Force at home is the responsibility of the Air Ministry, which allots appropriate tasks to commands. Commands decide upon a suitable policy and issue the necessary orders and instructions to groups. Groups in their turn decide upon the best action to take to implement the instructions passed down to them by commands and then issue appropriate orders to their wings or stations, who finally decide upon the detailed employment of the units. Thus as the broad orders and instructions originating from the Air Ministry pass down the chain of command each successive headquarters in turn elaborates them and re-transmits them in a suitable degree of detail to enable them to be acted upon by the next lower formation, until finally, precise and fully detailed operation orders or instructions are issued to the units. Similarly, when a unit or lower formation raises questions of operational policy these are transmitted upwards through successively higher formations until they reach a formation with a status sufficiently high to deal with them.

6. All operational matters are normally dealt with in this way and are passed up and down between formations and units without omitting any intermediate formation headquarters. The importance of not omitting an intermediate formation arises from the fact that the number of intermediate formations interposed between the Air Ministry and the units is determined by considering from an operational point of view the number, status and level of the intermediate formations that are required for the efficient control of the units. Thus, unless all operational matters pass up and down the operational control chain , without missing out any links, the operational control system will be incorrectly used and delays and uncertainties will result.
[...]

Control of Administrative Policy

11. As stated in para. 4 above, the number and status of the intermediate formations between the Air Ministry and the units are designed to meet the requirements of operational control. A natural consequence of this is that any matters of whatever nature which affect operations, must follow the same channels of communication between formations as do purely operational matters. Matters of administrative policy are therefore dealt with through the same channels of communication which are designed for operational control and are described in paras. 4–8. An exception to this is, however, made where the A.O.C. of an overseas command is responsible for operations to a Governor or a General Officer Commanding. When this is so matters of administrative policy above command level pass directly to and from the Air Ministry instead of to and from the Governor or the General Officers Commanding. The latter is, nevertheless, kept informed of all matters of administrative policy which may have repercussions upon the operational efficiency of the force.

12. Commanders of all formations must be given the opportunity of expressing their views on matters of administrative policy, both as regards personnel and material, which influence the operational capacity of their units. For this reason, commanders of all intermediate formations are provided with a policy staff (see Chapter III), capable of dealing not only with all operational matters but also with matters of administrative policy affecting operations.

Control of Matters of Administrative Routine

13. Para. 15 of section I of this chapter states that intermediate formations are only interposed where the number of junior formations or units becomes excessive for a single senior formation to control and administer efficiently. The number and status of the formations in the Royal Air Force are primarily designed to meet the requirements of operational control, and therefore, all operational matters and all administrative matters affecting operations, must go through each formation headquarters as they pass either up or down the chain. The same number of intermediate formations may not, however, be necessary in dealing with administrative routine duties which, provided they are efficiently and regularly discharged in accordance with general policy, are not immediately connected with the operational capacity of the units. It would cause unnecessary delay and would constitute a source of weakness to insist on matters of administrative routine passing through the same official channels as operational matters when it is not really necessary. The majority of matters of administrative routine are, therefore, dealt with as appropriate by administrative service organizations which are represented when necessary at intermediate formation headquarters.

Exercise of Control

14. The correct use of the systems of control described above is a matter of great importance to ensure that air forces function speedily and efficiently and to ensure that, whilst every individual in the organization is kept fully in touch with all matters that he must know about in order to discharge his duties properly, no person expends effort upon matters that do not concern him.

15. No rigid set of rules can be devised from which it will be possible to determine in any specific circumstances which channel should be used to deal with a particular Service problem. Individuals must be able to distinguish not only operational from administrative matters, but they must also be able to distinguish between matters of administrative policy and administrative routine. The guiding principle in determining by which channel any particular administrative matter should be despatched is whether or not it is a matter that affects or alters the operational capacity of units. If it does, it should normally go through each intermediate formation headquarters. If not, it may then follow an appropriate routine or administrative service channel, according to whether it is a personnel or a material matter. It is important for all personnel in any headquarters to study this aspect of organization and administration, so as to be able to use the machinery put at their disposal to its best advantage.

[. . .]

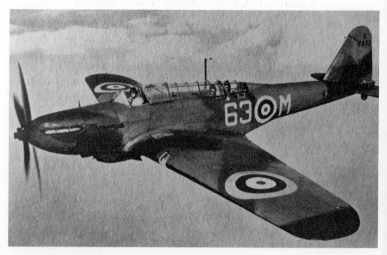

The Fairey Battle was a single-engine light bomber, with a three-man crew.

CHAPTER XI
INTELLIGENCE ORGANIZATION

The Object of Intelligence

1. Detailed knowledge of the relative strengths, armament, training and morale of the opposing forces, of the physical and climatic characteristics of the theatre of operations, and of the psychology of the enemy people, their national characteristics, resources and industrial and economic organization is essential to success in war.

2. The acquisition and distribution of this information, the object of which is to ensure the most effective employment of our forces, and the prevention of the acquisition of similar information by the enemy form the main duties of an intelligence organization.

3. In order to frame the best possible plan of campaign this knowledge must be in our possession prior to the outbreak of war, and the collection and study of such information in peace time is the combined task of the intelligence services of the Empire.

4. It is the duty of the Air Intelligence Branch of the Air Ministry to take the necessary measures in advance in peace time to acquire all the information which is likely to be required by air officers commanding in the field and on the outbreak of war to ensure that they are supplied with all the relevant information as it becomes available.

5. Apart from the information which will be required in regard to such subjects as the strength, composition, distribution and fighting qualities of the enemy's air forces, and an appreciation of the enemy commander's intentions, the Air Ministry will be responsible for the supply, where possible, of information in regard to objectives suitable for air attack.

6. The Air Intelligence Branch of the Air Ministry is therefore responsible for the collection, in collaboration with the other Services, of information regarding the enemy's naval, military and air organizations, and the communications, supply organization, industrial resources and administrative machinery upon which they depend. A study should also be made of objectives for air attack so that the branch may be in a position to assist in the selection of objectives, the attack of which will best serve the furtherance of the plan of campaign approved by His Majesty's Government.

Sources of Information

7. An intelligence organization with an Air Force in the field will be, to a certain extent, dependent for information upon the home organization, which will act as a

coordinating, collecting and distributing agency for intelligence obtained from all sources, departments, and other theatres of war outside the control of a commander in the field.

8. In addition to the intelligence which will be received, through the medium of the intelligence organizations at home or with allies, the following are the principal sources of information in the field. They are placed here in no special order of merit, as their relative value will vary according to circumstances, but the air and other fighting forces will form the chief collecting medium:—

   (i) Reports of enemy air activity, and casualties.
  (ii) Air reconnaissance and balloon observation.
 (iii) Air photographs and sketches.
 (iv) Reports and photographs from units of the result of attacks on enemy objectives.
  (v) Combat reports from units.
 (vi) Enemy signal organization and traffic.
(vii) Interception of enemy signals.
(viii) Interrogation of prisoners of war and civilians.
 (ix) Study of captured documents, of the hostile and neutral press, of military reports of areas, guide books, gazetteers and similar publications dealing with the theatre of operations, and the correspondence of prisoners of war.
  (x) Agents.
 (xi) Examination of captured aircraft and enemy equipment in general.

9. It is essential that all available channels through which information can be collected should be utilized, because no source of intelligence is complete or entirely reliable by itself, and if undue reliance is placed on information from any one source, there is a danger that false deductions may be made. Moreover, the enemy might utilise that particular source for the dissemination of false information, and the intelligence section must therefore confirm and check the information obtained with that obtained from other sources.

10. The organization and duties of the Intelligence Section of an Air or R.A.F. Headquarters in the field are dealt with in the following paragraphs under the three conditions under which Air Forces may be operating, as described in Chapter I, paragraph I of this Manual.

Duties of the Intelligence Section when the Air Force is Operating from a Base of its Own

11. An air intelligence section will form part of the air branch in the organization of an air headquarters in the field, and will work in close liaison with the operations section, the Air Intelligence Branch of the Air Ministry, and the intelligence

organizations of other services. The air intelligence section will be responsible for the collection, collation, and distribution of information concerning the enemy, the territory in his occupation, and his activities anywhere in the theatre of operations; for the denial to the enemy of all information about our own forces and the territory in our occupation; and also for certain other duties involved in those above, namely, security, censorship, publicity, and propaganda. As however it is not at present contemplated that the air intelligence section should normally undertake responsibility for security, censorship, publicity and propaganda, the Army would probably be asked to attach the necessary personnel for these duties. In the event of this not being possible arrangements for dealing with these aspects of intelligence would have to be improvised in accordance with the principles laid down below.

12. The nature of the duties of the intelligence personnel and the need for the rapid transmission of the information acquired by them requires that they should work to a great extent independently of the normal chain of command, even where air intelligence sections or their equivalent form an integral part of the staffs of subordinate formations or units.

13. Speed, accuracy and clearness are the three essentials of an intelligence report, and the main principle to be observed in distributing information is that the appropriate information shall reach the right people in time to be of the maximum value, and that it shall be presented to them in the most convenient form. The method of transmission of information will be by wireless, telegraph, telephone, despatch rider, aeroplane, or personal visit, according to circumstances, and in certain cases it may be necessary to call on the signal service to provide special intercommunication arrangements.

14. The air intelligence section will be divided into four sub-sections, dealing respectively with:—

  (i) Organization, administration and records.
  (ii) Information.
  (iii) Security.
  (iv) Censorship, publicity and propaganda.

The work of one or more sub-sections may, however, be combined, according to the nature of the campaign and the size of the intelligence staff. The duties of the head of the air intelligence section, and of the various sub-sections, are dealt with in detail below.

Duties of the Head of the Air Intelligence Section

15. Under the control of the Senior Air Staff officer, the head of the intelligence section at air headquarters will be responsible for organizing the service of intelligence

so as to ensure the collection, collation and distribution of all information obtainable in the field, and for co-ordinating if necessary by interchange of liaison officers the work of the air intelligence section with that of other British and allied naval, military, air and civil intelligence services and officials.

16. His first concern will be to ensure that the Senior Air Staff Officer is furnished with the information necessary to enable the Air Officer Commanding-in-Chief to frame his plans for operations, and in addition the main responsibility for deducing and forecasting the probable enemy lines of action will devolve upon him. He will also be responsible for the supply to subordinate commanders of all available information which may be of assistance to them in appreciating the local situation and in executing their share of the plan of operations.

Organization, Administration and Records

17. A large amount of work will be entailed in the air intelligence section in superintending the organization and conduct of intelligence duties, in studying intelligence policy, in dealing with the discipline and interior economy of intelligence personnel, and in distributing and recording the information received. The main headings under which the work of this sub-section will fall are as follows:—

  (i) General organization, co-ordination and administration of the air intelligence service.
 (ii) Intelligence appointments, records and registry.
(iii) Distribution and record of information received.
 (iv) Editing, printing and issue of intelligence reports, summaries and publications.
  (v) The supply and issue of maps. This is normally the responsibility of the Army, and when the Air Force is operating independently special arrangements for the supply of maps will have to be made with the War Office.

Information

18. The information sub-section will be the centre to which all information regarding the enemy and the theatre of war, or which is in any way likely to influence operations, will be passed for study and disposal. The officer in charge of this sub-section will be responsible for the constant study of the enemy situation as revealed by the latest information and for immediately bringing anything of importance to the notice of those concerned.

19. Throughout the course of a campaign, early, accurate and continuous information regarding the enemy's order of battle, movements, dispositions, and the most profitable objectives for air attack, will be of the utmost importance. The

following are the more important heads under which information is likely to be required, prior to and during the course of a campaign:-

(i) Political and commercial intelligence.

(ii) Strategical and tactical movements, plans and intentions.

(iii) Preparation, in collaboration with air defence formations, of track charts of enemy aircraft and of a hostile air activity map.

(iv) Order of battle of enemy air forces, including organization, location of units and air bases, and types and numbers of aircraft.

(v) Enemy's supply organization and communications.

(vi) Enemy air casualties, losses, wastage, reserves, and resources of air material and personnel.

(vii) The enemy anti-aircraft defences.

(viii) The psychology and national characteristics of the enemy and the temper of the inhabitants.

(ix) The topography and meteorological conditions of the theatre of operations.

(x) Repair facilities, details of equipment, development and performance of enemy aircraft.

(xi) Suspected developments in new methods of fighting (e.g., chemical warfare, wireless controlled aircraft).

(xii) Vulnerability of enemy to air attack—to include information concerning such objects as naval, military and air organizations, their communications, supply and transportation services, the industrial resources, power supply, imports, material and administrative machinery upon which they depend. Sufficient information must be available to ensure that the vulnerable points and weak links can be assessed and that suitable air objectives can be chosen and identified.

It is not possible in this chapter to define more closely the relative responsibility of the Air Ministry and of the Air Officer Commanding in the field for the collection of this information, since the division of responsibility rests to a great extent on the circumstances of the campaign.

(xiii) The material and moral effects of air attacks on enemy objectives.

(xiv) Enemy signal system, organization, equipment and traffic. Interception, translation and decyphering of enemy messages.

(xv) The enemy's intelligence personnel and methods.

20. Until the time that allies actually join with us in hostilities, responsibility for providing information concerning them will normally be the province of the air intelligence section, but when allies have actually joined us in the field, the maintenance of touch with them will normally devolve upon liaison officers or missions.

21. In order to simplify the duties of sifting and classifying the information received, it will sometimes be necessary, according to the nature of the campaign and the size of the air intelligence section, to sub-divide the information sub-section into two or more sub-divisions. In a major war there will usually be five of these sub-divisions, namely:

(i) Enemy intentions and operations.
(ii) Enemy order of battle, rear organization and defences, supplies and communications.
(iii) Enemy resources, repair and maintenance organization and technical development.
(iv) Vulnerability of enemy organizations to air attack.
(v) Enemy signals.

Under certain conditions an additional sub-division may be required to deal with interpretation of photographs.

The most vital part of the air-raid warning infrastructure was the Chain Home (CH) radar system, with 22 such radar stations dotted along the English southern and eastern coastline by the summer of 1940, the 350ft (106m) lattice masts standing out prominently in the countryside. These stations, which typically detected raids out to about 60 miles (97km) distance, were augmented by 30 Chain Home Low (CHL) radar, which could pick up low-flying aircraft, closing an important gap in the radar coverage. The CH and CHL networks gave Fighter Command an undeniable advantage in the Battle of Britain, enabling the fighter aircraft to be scrambled in response to actual raids, rather than conducting endless costly and inefficient standing patrols.

Technology had its limits, however, and the Observer Corps (OC) filled the gaps in the system capably. The OC can appear quaint to modern eyes, but during the Battle of the Britain and the subsequent Blitz they played a crucial role in the country's air defence. Its thousands of mainly civilian operators used eyesight, binoculars, mechanical instruments and even sound locator devices to identify and track raiding air units, transmitting vital information about bearing, altitude and force composition through to the various command centres. In the passage below, the references to the 'Observer Instrument' is to a mechanical sighting instrument, fitted to a gridded map, on which the enemy aircraft could be plotted.

From *Instructions for Observer Posts* (1941)

1. The System.—One of the first necessities defence is constant information of the number, course and height of hostile aircraft. In order to obtain this information, observer posts are organised over the whole country; these posts communicate their information by direct telephone lines to observer centres.

The system further provides that the information shall be quickly passed from the observer centres to the various air defence commanders.

It also provides the information needed for air raid warnings, but the issue of warnings is not an Observer Corps responsibility.

2. The Observer Post.—Each observer post is called by a letter and number – A1, A2, A3, B1, B2, etc. The strength of each post should be sufficient to ensure continuous manning by two observers, working in reliefs.

3. Equipment.—Each observer post is equipped with the articles shown in Appendix.

Should any of them require repair or replacement, a postcard stating what is required should be sent direct to:–

The Observer Group Officer, in whose group the Post lies. N.B.—Small repairs to the telephone instrument can be arranged for by the Head Observer direct with the local Post Office authority.

4. Setting up of the Observer Instrument.—In war-time, the Instrument Table is permanently set up in the look-out. When set up, the top of the table should be level, and it is most important that the chart should be oriented true North and South. To do this, the bearing of a distant prominent object is marked by an arrow on the chart. In order to set the chart, the circular table should be moved round until the arrow is pointing to this prominent object. The table should then be clamped in this position.

The setting of the chart may be checked by reference to the sun at noon (G.M.T.) or the Pole Star at night.

A nearby object on the line of bearing of the aiming mark should be noted, so that on a dark night (when no stars are visible) the Chart can be re-set if turned accidentally.

5. The states of readiness of the Observer Corps in war-time are:–
Stage 1–"Readiness."
This stage will represent the full manning of all Centres and Posts, the two men at the Posts being actually on the look-out.
Stage 2–"Available."
In this stage the crew of two men should be at each Post, but one may be resting in the shelter or elsewhere, provided he remains within earshot of the telephone bell. The Observer Instrument should be erected and covered, and one man must be on the look-out. All communications remain switched

through. The conditions under the AVAILABLE must be such that the Group can be at READINESS within the number of minutes ordered.

6. *(a)* The telephone is permanently connected up in wartime.

Make sure that the microphone switch is kept in the off position except when speaking.

Note.—The microphone switch is operated by moving the mouthpiece. The switch is "on" when the mouthpiece is opposite the mouth for speaking, and "off" when the mouthpiece is turned downwards to its fullest extent. (See instructions contained inside the telephone.)

(b) The telephone is placed on the ground underneath the observer instrument. The front of the box should be closed except when it is necessary to ring the centre.

(c) The ringing arrangements to the centre should be tested regularly. The plotter will say "Test ring please" and No. 2 will then turn the generator handle on the front of the telephone sharply. The plotter at the centre will report if his bell has rung correctly.

The plotter at the centre will then test the ringing at the observer post and No. 2 observer will report whether the bell has rung correctly.

(d) Should it not be possible to communicate with the centre, use should be made of the nearest available telephone to ring up the centre whose telephone number is given on the chart and inform the centre that the line to the post is out of order. The centre will then be responsible for taking action with the Post Office and, if necessary, will arrange for a Post Office linesman to be sent out to put matters right.

The cost of the telephone call will be refunded on being reported to the Observer Group Officer.

[. . .]

An air observer in London scans the skies for enemy aircraft.

7. Method of observing and reporting.

(i) *(a)* **Duties.**—No. 1 observer on duty is responsible for the general working of the observer post. He is to watch and listen for the aircraft, and, in the case of visible aircraft, will estimate the height and set the estimated height on the height column by turning the milled edged screw.

He will align the sighting arm on the aircraft by sliding or traversing the movable carriage towards or away from him, using either the "open" sight on top of the sighting arm, or tubular cross-wire sight.

No. 2 observer on duty, working under the general direction of No. 1, will act as telephonist and report to the centre the position of the aircraft read from the chart, as shown by the pointer on the sliding carriage.

No. 2 will listen for plots sent in by neighbouring posts and, where possible, use these to obtain "corrected" heights (see para. 8).

When the aircraft cannot be seen, but is mostly heard, No. 1 will proceed as detailed in sub-para. (iv). It is essential that, in this case, a "sound" plot should be given.

Note.–The work of an observer post equipped with the IIb or c type instrument can, if necessary, be carried out by one observer acting alone, but two observers should always be on duty.

(b) **Low Flying Aircraft.**—When planes are flying below about 2,000 ft. it is not practicable to use the Observer instrument. In such cases No. 1 of the Post must estimate their position and place his finger on the square. No. 2 will report this square as if it had been obtained in the normal manner, and give the estimated direction of flight and height.

(The scale of a Post Chart is:—one inch represents one mile.)

(Each square is 2 km. square. 2 km. = 1¼ m. approx.)

(ii) **Form of Reports.**—*(a)* When No. 1 reports that his sights are "On," No. 2 will read off the chart the square indicated by the pointer.

(b) No. 2 will then report to the observer centre in the following form, first giving the letter and number of his post: "B2 calling, plane (or planes) seen, 6153."

(c) As soon as it can be ascertained he will rep ort the direction of flight, for example:—"Plane (or planes) seen 6153 flying North."

(d) If there are more aircraft than one, he will substitute the number of planes as soon as these can be counted, stating whether in formation.

(e) When the main information is through, supplementary information should be given, including the height, whether estimated or corrected (see para. 8), at which the aircraft are flying, and, if the post is able to recognise the aircraft as enemy or friendly, this should also be stated. If unable to recognise it or them, the Post should state "unrecognised," and if thought to be "hostile" should say so.

(f) A typical report would, therefore, be in the following terms:—

"B2 calling, three planes seen 6153 flying North, height 8,000 ft." and when through:–

"8,000 ft. is estimated (or corrected) height," followed by information as to type of plane, e.g., Friendly Bomber or Fighter, Hostile, or unrecognised, and, if recognised:—Wellington or Dornier (for example).

(g) If there is no marked alteration in course or height subsequent reports should be given in the following manner:—"B2 calling same plane(s) now 6357, corrected height (if obtained) 9,000 ft." "Recognised as ...."

(iii) **Number and Frequency of Reports.**—Too frequent reporting by posts causes confusion and delay at the centre, and must therefore be avoided. The plotter will regulate the reporting by Posts. Especial care should be taken to make the following reports:

(a) On first sighting or hearing an aircraft. This fact should immediately be reported to the centre, together with a plot. Centre will say if plots are required outside the post's area.

(b) Directly an aircraft comes on to the post chart, regular reporting is to commence.

(c) Thereafter every alternate square so long as the aircraft remains on a straight course and on the post chart.

(d) When about to pass overhead and when overhead.

(e) Immediately before the aircraft passes out of sight or off the post chart, whichever happens first.

(f) Any marked change in the course or height of the aircraft during its transit.

One of the Chain Home radar stations, the most important component amongst the British air defence technologies.

(iv) **Reporting of Aircraft by Sound**.—*(a)* Plots *must* be given of aircraft heard although they cannot be seen. The fact that plots thus obtained may be somewhat inaccurate is of no importance compared with the necessity of making a ready report to the centre, giving a 'sound' plot which shows the **direction** in which the aircraft is **heard** by the post.

(b) The method adopted is the use of a 'sound' circle of 5 miles radius marked in blue on the chart and labelled 'sound circle'. All sound plots other than the 'overhead' report are given on this circle. If the post is able to estimate by ear the direction from which the sound appears to come, No. 1 will set the pointer of the instrument on the sound circle and point the instrument in this direction.

No. 2 observer will then report a plot on **the sound circle** in this direction, whether the aircraft appears to be far or near, stressing the word "heard," e.g. "plane heard, 3.30 at 10,000" (3.30 being the nearest half-hour by the clock code on the sound circle). The actual position of the aircraft, and, in time, its track, is worked out at the centre from the information given by plots from posts.

Therefore, the whole of the time that the plane is audible, reports at regular intervals must be given to the centre unless the plotter at the centre says they are not required. If the direction of sound remains the same, repetition of the same plot indicates to the centre that the plane is flying directly towards or away from the post reporting and this assists the centre in ascertaining the direction of flight.

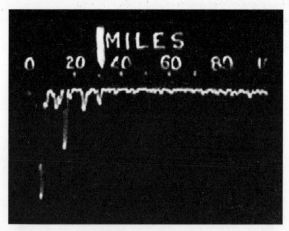

The operator's screen of a Chain Home radar.

The Army's Anti-Aircraft Command, as noted above, fell under the direction of RAF Fighter Command. The Command was divided into a Command HQ and seven regional 'Divisions', each with varying allocations of guns and manpower. The main types of anti-aircraft gun used during the Battle of Britain were the 40mm Bofors, mainly for firing on fast, low-flying aircraft such as fighters and dive-bombers, and 3in, 3.7in and 4.5in guns for high-altitude targets. The extract here comes from a US Navy wartime manual that explains some of the universal principles of operating the Bofors guns.

From *40 MM Antiaircraft Gun*, OP 820 (1943)

Chapter IV
CYCLIC OPERATION

Cyclic Operation of The Gun Mechanism

In automatic fire, one complete cycle of operation occurs approximately every half second. In each cycle the following basic functions are performed:

A live round is fed onto the tray.
The rammer is cocked.
The round is rammed into the barrel chamber. The breech is closed.
The round is fired.
The empty case is ejected.

These basic functions are shown step by step in the following diagrams, following a round through the complete cycle from feeding to ejection. In these diagrams, the cool colors (green and blue) are used to indicate the parts of the gun mechanism that move in recoil, while the warm colors (red, orange, and yellow) are used to indicate other moving parts.

A. FEEDING THE ROUND

The barrel assembly, breech mechanism, and tray are moving forward in counterrecoil. The breech block is held down by the extractors, and the rammer shoe is held back by the tray catch lever. The star wheels are released, the catch heads of the catch mechanisms having been tripped by the rammer tray pawls. The feed pawls, due to the action of the tray guides, are pressing the rounds down. This forces the bottom round between the star wheels and onto the tray.

B. COCKING THE RAMMER

The barrel assembly, breech mechanism, and tray are still moving forward in counterrecoil and have almost reached battery position. The live round is now on the tray with its base in the slots of the rammer levers. The rammer shoe is being held back by the tray catch lever, and as the tray moves forward, the rammer spring is compressed, cocking the rammer. The trigger catch lever is held down by the trigger mechanism, and the loader catch lever is held down by the rounds in the loader. This leaves only the tray catch lever holding the rammer shoe.

C. RAMMING THE ROUND

The parts that were moving forward in counterrecoil have now reached battery position. The beveled cam on the under side of the tray has ridden over the forward end of the rocker arm, tripping the tray catch lever, thus allowing the rammer shoe and levers to be thrown forward by the action of the rammer spring. As the rammer levers neared the forward limit of their travel, they were spread apart by the cam slots of the tray through which they extend. This allows the round to continue its travel and be thrown into the barrel chamber.

D. CLOSING THE BREECH

The round is completely in the chamber and the closing spring is raising the breech block to the closed position. The breech block is free to rise, because the extractors were unhooked from the block by the base of the round as it was thrown into the chamber. As the block rises, pressure of the cam on the left inner crank is removed from the outer cocking lever. The firing pin is being held back only by the inner cocking lever which is prevented from moving by the sear.

E. FIRING THE ROUND

The breech is completely closed and the round is fired. Firing occurs after the breech is closed, by the action of the cam of the right inner crank upon the sear. The cam forces the sear inward, releasing the inner cocking lever and the firing pin. The firing pin strikes the primer, which explodes the propellant charge of the round.

F. EJECTING THE CASE

The barrel assembly, breech mechanism, and tray are moving rearward as a result of the momentum imparted by the powder pressure at the beginning of recoil. The breech block is in the open position, the outer and inner cranks having been rotated by action of the roller, riding against the cam surface of the side door. The firing pin is cocked by action of the cam of the left inner crank depressing the outer cocking lever. As the breech block descended, it struck the toes of the extractors, ejecting the empty case. The feed pawls, due to the action of the tray guides, are rising in order to feed the next round onto the tray.

A complete cycle has now taken place, and the action repeats itself in automatic fire as long as the loader is supplied with ammunition and the trigger mechanism is held in the firing position.

A 40mm Bofors gun being towed into position.

Chapter VI
LOADING AND UNLOADING

A. INSTRUCTIONS FOR LOADING

1. Put the firing selector lever on SAFE.

2. Move the hand operating lever all the way to the rear, then latch it in the rear catch bracket.

3. Push a full clip into the loader, so that one round drops onto the rammer tray. When the clip is pushed in far enough to accomplish this, the empty clip will be ejected through the clip chute. Place another full clip in the loader.

4. Move the hand operating lever forward and latch it in the forward catch bracket.

5. See that the feed control thumb lever on the loader rear guide, if provided, is in the position indicated by the red arrow.

6. Place the firing selector lever on AUTO FIRE or SINGLE FIRE as desired.

7. a. Hold the firing pedal of the mount down for automatic fire.
   b. Press the firing pedal smartly for each shot in single fire.

8. Keep the loader filled.

The loader catch lever will stop operation, with the rammer shoe cocked, when only two rounds remain, one on the tray and one on the star wheels. The gun mechanism is then in condition to resume automatic fire when the loader is refilled, without further manipulation of the hand operating lever.

B. INSTRUCTIONS FOR UNLOADING

1. Place the firing selector lever on SAFE.

2. Elevate the gun to about 30 degrees.

3. Move the hand operating lever all the way to the rear, making sure an assistant catches the live round thus released from the rammer levers, as the round slides through the opening in the rear door.

4. Place the hand operating lever in the rear catch bracket.

5. Install the round releasing tool (298899) in the side frames, compressing the feed and stop pawls.

6. Lift out the rounds which have been released. Remove the round releasing tool.

7. Using the pusher tool (298876), force the round on the star wheels down on to the rammer tray. Remove the round.

8. Move the hand operating lever fully forward to release the star wheel catch mechanisms, and then latch it in the rear catch bracket.

9. Use the pusher tool to force the last round through the star wheels on to the tray. Remove the round as before.

10. When the loader is empty, secure the hand operating lever in the forward catch bracket. Trip the extractors with the extractor release lever to close the breech block.

11. Depress the feed control lever in the rear guide and then release it. This operation will release the rammer shoe from the loader catch lever. Place the firing selector lever at either firing position. Press the firing pedal of the mount smartly to release the rammer shoe from the trigger catch lever.

12. Place the firing selector lever on SAFE.

CHAPTER 3
AIR COMBAT TACTICS

The arena of fighter air combat was utterly unforgiving. The pilot's skill in handling the aircraft was just one element, albeit a critical one, in his survival. Survival also depended upon factors such as the aircraft's inherent performance (ranking in importance to airmanship), its ability to absorb combat damage, the weather conditions, and the speed at which the squadrons were 'scrambled' in response to a raid. (The earlier they received notification of the raid, the quicker they could take off and the greater altitude they could therefore attain; relative altitude often translated to combat advantage, as much of the killing was done in the first fast, diving pass). There was also an unnerving amount of luck involved – one poorly aimed snatched burst of machine-gun or cannon fire could still end the receiving pilot's flight, or life, abruptly.

Within the RAF, the development of air combat tactics was at first heavily constrained by tradition and hidebound thinking. Fighter Command had codified its tactical doctrine in the 1938 *Manual of Air Tactics*. In this book, the core tactical formation for fighter aircraft was the three-fighter 'Vic', a forward-pointing 'V' configuration led by a section leader at the front and two wingmen positioned close behind and either side. The 12 aircraft of a squadron would organise themselves in four Vics. The advantage of the Vic was that it enabled the fighters to stay in close proximity to one another, especially in bad weather, and to coordinate their offensive fire against enemy bombers, which were the main consideration when the tactic was developed, not fast-moving and fluid enemy fighters. It had, therefore, a crucial flaw – the two wingmen spent more of their time formation flying in relation to the section leader than scanning the surrounding sky for threats. This flaw was cruelly exposed during the early stages of the Battle of Britain, when the RAF pilots came up against the German *Schwarm* formations, which consisted of four aircraft made up of two pairs, staggered in altitude and position so that each pair, and each individual, had good all-round observation, and with enough distance between them to avoid the need for close formation flying. In action, these pairs could break off on their own, the leader and wingman fighting as a mutually protective unit. Slowly seeing the sense of this formation, the RAF gradually began to adopt a similar formation, the 'finger four', although it took some time to push through the resistance to change.

In this chapter, we bring together a multitude of documents relating to the development of air tactics during the Battle of Britain. We start with a short list of rules by the South African pilot Adolph Gysbert 'Sailor' Malan, one of the great RAF fighter aces of World War II, who scored 27 individual kills and seven joint kills. His presence in this book reminds us that Britain owned a debt of gratitude to pilots of many different nationalities, including Poles, Czechs, Canadians and New Zealanders, who flew into combat alongside native Britons at a time when the UK needed them most.

From Sailor Malan, 'Ten of My Rules for Air Fighting' (1940)

1. Wait until you see the whites of his eyes. Fire short bursts of 1 to 2 seconds and only when your sights are definitely "ON".

2. Whilst shooting think of nothing else, brace the whole of the body, have both hands on the stick, concentrate on your ring sight.

3. Always keep a sharp lookout. "Keep your finger out!"

4. Height gives you the initiative.

5. Always turn and face the attack.

6. Make your decisions promptly. It is better to act quickly even though your tactics are not the best.

7. Never fly straight and level for more than 30 seconds in the combat area.

8. When diving to attack always leave a proportion of your formation above to act as top guard.

9. INITIATIVE, AGGRESSION, AIR DISCIPLINE, and TEAM WORK are the words that MEAN something in Air Fighting.

10. Go in quickly – Punch hard – Get out!

Supermarine Spitfires flying in close formation.

From 'Hints and Tips for Fighter Pilots' (July 1940)

TACTICS OF ENEMY ESCORT

The enemy escorting fighters normally maintain their formation and position until our fighters start to attack the enemy bombers. Enemy fighters then immediately peel off in ones or twos in succession and dive very steeply upon our fighters. They open fire in the dive but do not usually attempt to remain on the tail of our fighters; instead, they continue their dive straight past and below and then climb up again into position for another attack.

TACTICS TO BE EMPLOYED AGAINST ENEMY FORMATIONS

Fighters should never rush in to attack a formation immediately after it is sighted. It is absolutely essential that the situation should be weighed up so that the most profitable method of attack can be decided upon, and also so that the disposition of the enemy fighters which are escorting the bombers may be studied. It must be remembered that the main aim is to shoot down the bombers; experience has proved that this cannot be done and that our fighters will be at a tactical disadvantage unless the enemy fighters are neutralised.

If, therefore, we have a strong force of fighters, at least a quarter of them must be detached to take up the attention of the enemy fighters so that, while they are thus occupied, the remainder of our fighters can attack the enemy bombers without interruption.

If, however, our fighters are numerically inferior to the enemy escorting fighters, some form of stratagem must be employed. Suggested methods are:

(a) Attack or feint attack with small part of our force against the enemy fighters so as to draw them off.

(b) That the fighter should make a feint attack upon the bombers, thus bringing down the enemy fighters against him. Close watch should be kept upon the fighter as it dives and just before it arrives within range, its attack should be avoided by quick manoeuvre. Time may thus be gained for a very quick attack upon the bombers before the next fighter arrives within firing range.

(c) A detachment manoeuvre above or to the flank of the enemy fighters to give warning by radio when enemy fighters start their attacking dive.

(d) Even a small detachment which reaches a position above the enemy fighters will often cause them to desert the bombers.

(e) If interference from enemy fighters can be temporarily neglected, a flight of five (see para f) aircraft can use the 'astern attack from the beam'. Aircraft take position in line astern, 800 yards to port of the enemy bomber formation, and ahead and 1,000ft above, on the order 'turn to right in astern. Going down', the flight turns in simultaneously. Nos 1 and 2 deliver a full beam attack, Nos 3 and 4 a quarter attack, fighters break away to the left and downwards, reform line astern to port of the formation, and repeat the manoeuvre.

(f) Our fighters have generally attacked enemy bombers from astern. The introduction of armour in enemy bombers may force us to attack from the beam and even from directly ahead. Such attacks are more difficult to deliver but have been frequently adopted and when properly executed, have been extremely successful.

DO NOTS

(a) Do not go into the middle of a vic of enemy bombers. If you do this they can concentrate the fire or their rear guns upon you. Attack them from the flank and if possible, from both flanks simultaneously.

(b) When you are going into the attack, do not give the enemy a chance of a deflection shot at you. As far as you can, keep your nose on the enemy, and approach in his blind spots as much as possible.

(c) Do not fire a long burst if enemy fighters are about; two seconds is long enough. Then break away quickly to ensure that an enemy fighter is not about to attack you. If all is clear, then you can immediately renew your attack upon the bomber.

(d) Do not break away by means of a climbing turn. This gives an easy shot to the enemy rear gunner. Break away outwards and downwards at as high a relative speed as possible.

(e) If the enemy forms a circle, do not attack it in a hesitating manner. When you attack a circle go straight into it without hesitation as soon as you can find a gap.

(f) Do not forget that enemy fighters can reach practically any part of this country. Never relax your vigilance.

PATROLLING

(a) Make certain before leaving the ground that you thoroughly understand the orders for the patrol and what you are expected to do.

(b) If your patrol is ordered to take off at a fixed time, be ready in plenty of time so that you can sit quietly and calmly in your aircraft, collecting your thoughts, before you have to take off.

(c) In choosing a height for your patrol, always try to patrol higher than the enemy.

A Heinkel He 111 passes over the Thames in central London during a bomber raid.

(d) Never patrol in tight formation. Two-five spans is a comfortable distance which allows you to search around without fear of collision.

(e) The rear aircraft or section of any fighter formation must always be in a position to watch the sky astern of the formation and to give warning of attacks by enemy fighters. If aircraft are in a single composite formation, the rear two aircraft should continually 'weave', i.e. swing across and exchange places with each other so that they can keep this watch to the rear. All aircraft in the formation, however, should try to assist in watching the whole sky.

(f) A useful patrol formation for a squadron is sections in line astern, stepped up, the third section to a flank and the rear section acting as look-out to the rear. Alternatively, aircraft have successfully patrolled in flights of five, each five forming an independent unit under its own leader. The look-out is provided by Nos 4 and 5 crossing over above the formation. On sighting the enemy formation, No. 4 or 5 dives down in front of the leader, indicating the position of the enemy by clock code over the R/T. As soon as he is in front of the formation, he turns off in the direction of the enemy. When the formation leader spots the enemy, he reassumes the leadership. If more than one flight of five operates together, No. 1 flight takes position above and to the flank of No. 2 Flight, each flight providing its own look-out.

(g) The same section should not be detailed to act as look-out for the whole period of the patrol because its 'weaving' tactics use up considerably more petrol than normal straight flying.

(h) Do not patrol continuously along the same track. This will allow enemy fighters to anticipate your movements and obtain a favourable position for a surprise attack on you.

(i) When patrolling, change your height and course continuously to avoid anti-aircraft fire.

(j) If you are patrolling, as you should, with a portion of your force acting as an upper guard, this guard should regulate its movements so that it can immediately go to the assistance of the lower formation when required.

(k) Never leave your formation unless ordered to do so.

ENEMY DECOY TACTICS

If you see a lone bomber apparently without any particular employment, he will almost certainly be a decoy, and fighters, 4,000ft above and probably hidden in the sun, are waiting for you to attack him. A favourite trick of enemy fighters is to allow one or two of their number to lead you just under clouds. When they have got you in that position, enemy fighters in superior numbers dive out of the clouds to attack you. Always expect that enemy fighters are in the offing and are waiting for you to take some unguarded action.

ENEMY FIGHTER TACTICS

(a) Me 109s and Me 110s normally fly in squadron formations of twelve.

(b) Enemy fighters always like to be in superior numbers and to have the advantage of height and sun. Unless they have these advantages, they will not usually stay to fight, but will make a quick diving attack hoping they have you at a disadvantage and will then use their speed to escape.

(c) German fighters often work in pairs. If you get on the tail of one, the other immediately tries to get on your tail.

(d) When attacked, German fighters will very often dive vertically away from you. It is not usually worthwhile to follow them especially if they are faster in the dive than you are. If you are over German territory he may try to lead you over a FLAK [anti-aircraft] battery.

(e) The Me 110, after he has attacked, will often pull up into a stall turn, so that he may have a look round to see where he should go next. If you can catch him at the top of his zoom, he is very easily shot down.

(f) The Me 110 will often make a head-on attack at you, and open fire with cannons at long range. He does not like to hold on to this attack to close range.

German Bf 109 fighters approach the combat area in staggered formation, each pilot scanning the skies for the enemy.

DOGFIGHT HINTS

(a) Formations quickly become broken up in a dogfight. Aircraft of sections should try, as far as possible, to keep together for mutual support.

(b) If you hear the sound of firing, turn immediately. The sound almost certainly comes from an enemy fighter which is attacking you from astern.

(c) Turn sharply and slightly downwards. Hurricanes and Spitfires are more manoeuvrable than German fighters and they will have difficulty following you in your turn. The Me 109 is particularly bad at a sharp turn to the right.

(d) If you are involved in a head-on attack, remember the rule of the air: when you have to break away to avoid collision, turn to the right.

(e) Never waste ammunition. The golden opportunity may come when your ammunition is finished.

(f) Be especially careful at the moment you break off a combat. Take evasive action immediately because you are especially liable to attack at this moment. A useful manoeuvre to break off a combat is a dive using full aileron. Regain height as soon as possible.

(g) If your engine stops dive straight down to make the enemy think that he has 'got' you. Manoeuvre without engine gives the game away and the enemy likes to concentrate on the 'lame duck'.

(h) If you have to bale out, half-roll on to your back, open the lid, undo your straps and push the stick forward.

(i) Never fly straight, particularly if you are alone. Keep continually turning from side to side so that you can keep a look-out behind you. If the sun is bright and is behind you, it is advisable to make a 360-degree turn at short intervals so that you can make quite certain that the sky is clear in all directions.

(j) Beware of the Hun in the Sun.

The object in night fighting is to 'stalk' the enemy and to reach firing position without being observed. The following points should be noted:

(a) Under normal conditions of darkness, aircraft which are not illuminated by searchlights can best be spotted when they are between 40-deg and 60-deg above you.

(b) Cockpit and instrument lighting should be reduced to the barest minimum to assist you in searching for the enemy, and to prevent your own presence being revealed.

(c) The illuminated ring sight should be dimmed so it is only just visible.

(d) Before opening fire the aircraft must be positively identified as an enemy. This is best achieved from a position below him.

(e) The following method of attack is recommended by Fighter Command. Having reached a position below the enemy and regulated your speed to his, slightly raise the nose of your aircraft without increasing the throttle opening; you will thus rise behind the enemy. Keep below his slipstream – if you have difficulty in holding your aircraft out of the slipstream it is usually an indication that you have reached too great a range.

(f) The range at which the enemy is engaged should be as short as possible; in no circumstances should it be greater than 150yd.

GENERAL HINTS

(a) If there is a chance that enemy fighters may be about, look well before you take off, turn quickly, be especially careful while circling the aerodrome before landing and do not make a long straight approach.

(b) Light AA guns from the ground are accurate and effective up to 4,000ft. The most dangerous heights for heavy AA guns are between 4,000ft and 8,000ft.

(c) Watch that your oxygen fittings do not come adrift.

(d) Do not leave your transmitter on 'send'. If you do, you make communication impossible for the whole formation and you may ruin the patrol.

(e) Remember to turn on your sight, and cine-camera on, if you have one.

(f) If you have been in action, test your hydraulic system for possible damage before you get back to your home aerodrome.

(g) If you see white or greyish smoke pouring out of an engine of the enemy aircraft, it probably means that you have damaged his cooling or oil circulation. You should therefore switch your aim to the other engine. Black smoke may indicate either that the engine has been damaged or that the pilot is overboosting. There are indications that the enemy will try to produce smoke artificially so as to deceive you, so you must use your judgement as to whether you have caused sufficient damage to make it impossible for him to return to his base.

FINALLY
Remember that the closer the range, the more certain you are of bringing down the enemy. Remember also that everyone tends to underestimate range and that when you think you are within 200yd of the enemy you are probably still 400yd away.

Tracer bullets leave trails of smoke as British fighters engage two German He 111s.

From 'Enemy Fighter Tactics' (1940)

ENEMY FIGHTER TACTICS.

1. With reference to Headquarters, Bomber Command letter BC/S.22560/Air dated 14th January, 1940, para. 8, further trials have now been carried out with a Flight of Wellingtons from No. 99 Squadron and two single Spitfires from No. 65 Squadron.

2. To date, for reasons of weather and other commitments, No. 37 Squadron has been unable to carry out trials at this station. The Squadron has arranged to do so at the earliest opportunity.

3. The Wellingtons flew at an indicated air speed of 140 m.p.h., and the Spitfires registered an indicated air speed of a little over 300 m.p.h. during the attacks. The heights of the exercises varied between 2,000 and 4,000 feet.

4. The Officer Commanding No. 99 Squadron said that the attacks as delivered by the Spitfires were practically identical as regards method with those of the Messerschmitt 110s. On the morning of the 22nd January, weather conditions were met similar to those experienced on 14th December, when Messerschmitt 110's were encountered, and the Officer Commanding No. 99 Squadron is of the opinion that the speed of the Spitfires was very much the same as that of the Messerschmitt 110s. It therefore appears likely that the 110s attacked at a speed of a little over 300 m.p.h., as opposed to 400 m.p.h. which was suggested by personnel engaged in operations on 18th December.

5. During these attacks, turns were made towards and away from the attacking aircraft and the Officer Commanding No. 99 Squadron is strongly of the opinion that the bombers should only turn towards the fighters. It is agreed that when the fighters approach from the astern to deliver beam attack, turning away makes their attack more difficult to deliver, but it has been established from these trials that turning towards the fighters enables the bombers to bring their front guns into action on practically every occasion. Also, turns towards the fighter do not necessitate such large alterations of course.

6. Therefore, the recommendations contained in para. 6 of the above-mentioned letter, which concerned Blenheim aircraft only, are modified in the light of these further trials to the effect that bombers with movable front guns should always turn towards the attacking fighters. The best time for the bombers to initiate the turn is when the fighter appears to be coming into the position from which he will deliver his attack. (The Officer Commanding No. 99 Squadron is of the opinion that an experienced Fighting Controller will readily decide this point). When the fighter approached across the front of the bombers' formation prior to turning in

to attack, the bombers turn was begun as soon as he has passed the straight ahead position. By 'nosing' on to the fighter, the fighter was completely misplaced for a beam attack.

7. During these trials, the bombers adopted a special formation which will hereafter be referred to as the "99 Formation". [. . .] The Officer Commanding No. 99 Squadron claims that he has thus achieved a formation in which there are literally no stragglers, those aircraft that are on the outside of the formation having others behind them and those that are behind having others on the outside of them. It will also be noted that the general line of the formation is diagonally from starboard down to port, and that the maximum variety of levels that can be expected from aircraft in a formation has been obtained. It is also claimed by the Officer Commanding No. 99 Squadron that this formation is a very suitable one from which to carry out bombing.

8. The fighters found that on approaching this formation, it was quite difficult to determine its shape and accurately to memorise the position of an individual aircraft, if through turns it had to be temporarily lost to view.

9. At first, in the opinion of this Unit, the "99 Formation" was rather wide and would permit a number of enemy aircraft to attack at once from the rear. Later, with more experience, the formation became compact. There is a tendency for inexperienced pilots on the left hand side of the formation to swing out on turns and so become isolated.

10. The Squadron attempted during part of the trials to use the Box formation but did not like it, stating that it was difficult and dangerous to maintain, the reasons being that the aircraft on the left having the pilots on the left of their own aircraft cannot see to maintain their positions. This resulted particularly in the top section of the box being really wide and the left hand pilot being unable to see the remainder when turning to the left.

11. The films taken by the fighter aircraft show that close beam attacks present snap shooting opportunities only and that there are definite possibilities of aircraft other than those aimed at being hit.

12. With reference to the value of the beam attack to the fighter, it must be emphasised that the Wellingtons are reduced to flying at a speed of 140 m.p.h. Even with the bombers flying at this speed, it is felt that the expectation of favourable results cannot be high but that the attack might be used occasionally against bombers with strong tail armament, or to take advantage of the sun. In the opinion of the fighter pilots who carried out the attacks, a certain amount of pervious training is required to do so efficiently. It is particularly noticeable that the greater the margin of speed between the fighter and the bomber, the easier it is to deliver the attack.

13. Further trials of Spitfires delivering beam attacks against faster flying aircraft will be carried out at an early date.

14. From discussion with the Officer Commanding No. 99 Squadron, it appears that due to the effective Wellington rear armament, the enemy fighters have had to abandon the astern attack. Should the enemy bombers increase their rear armament or armour, it may be considered necessary for our fighters to deliver attacks from positions other than astern.

(SGD). H.F. VINCENT
Wing Commander,
Commanding, A.F.D.U.

AFDU/3/19/Air.
23rd January, 1940.

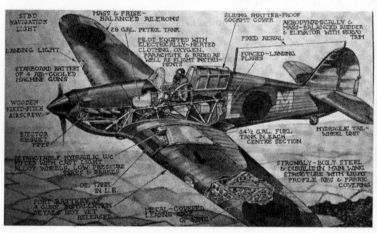

A cutaway diagram of the Hawker Hurricane.

From 'Tactical information gained from German Air Force attacks on R.A.F. Aerodromes' (1940)

SECRET   T.C.9.

Tactical information gained from German
Air Force attacks on R.A.F. Aerodromes.

The daylight attacks on R.A.F. aerodromes which have been carried out since the beginning of August, 1940 have resulted in certain tactical information regarding the methods of attack, and the lessons learnt from them, becoming available.

METHODS OF ATTACK

2. Broadly speaking, the methods of attack, when more than one aircraft are engaged, have fallen into one of the following categories:–

Steep Dive Bombing Attack:

(a) This type of attack is carried out in clear weather conditions by formations of Ju.87's or Me.110's, varying in number from 12 to 30 aircraft. These formations approach the aerodrome at medium altitude (e.g. 7,000 ft.) in close vic formation. Breaking off, one by one, the aircraft dive steeply, release their bombs at a low altitude and occasionally machine gun the aerodrome when pulling out of the dive. These formations will normally be preceded or accompanied by formations of fighters at high altitude, which will either circle the aerodrome while the bombing attack takes place, or attempt to distract and engage any of our own patrolling fighters which may be in the vicinity.

Shallow Dive Bombing Attack:

(b) This type of attack is carried out both in clear and cloudy weather, by formations of Me.110, Do.17, Do.215 or Ju.88. In clear weather fighter escorts usually accompany the bombers as in (a), but in cloudy weather the bombers are likely to be in smaller formations and unescorted. The aircraft descend in shallow dives as low as 400 ft. to release their bombs, and machine gun the aerodrome at the same time.

Low Level Attack.

(c) This type of attack normally takes place at 300 ft. by the small formations of about 5 aircraft, flying in tight vic formation. Inland aerodromes will probably experience this form of attack when adequate low cloud cover prevails; but coastal aerodromes are likely to be attacked from seaward in clear weather also.

TARGETS

3. Recent experience, which is supported by statements and diaries of prisoners of war, has shown that these attacks have invariably been directed against aerodrome

buildings, and hangars in particular. The landing ground and dispersed aircraft have not been the primary object.

DEDUCTIONS

4. If these attacks can be taken as representative of the enemy's policy when attacking aerodromes, the deductions which may be drawn therefrom are:

(a) In clear weather, large scale dive bombing attacks can be expected, accompanied by fighter escorts.
(b) In cloudy weather, shallow diver or low level attacks on a smaller scale can be expected.
(c) The primary task of the enemy fighter escort is to engage or draw off our fighter patrols at high altitudes, while diver bombers attack from lower altitudes.
(d) Attacks are always organised and times with the intention of achieving surprise, and are executed with the greatest precision and rapidity. Surprise if often achieved by raids, which are apparently approaching one objective, splitting up or changing direction suddenly, and attacking an entirely different target from that apparently indicated.
(e) Aerodrome buildings and hangars in particular are regarded by the enemy as more important than landing areas and dispersed aircraft.

SOME RECOMMENDATIONS FOR AERODROME DEFENCE.

5. (a) To avoid the effects of surprise, aerodrome ground defences must be on the alert at all times.
(b) Ground defences should be so disposed as to afford the maximum protection to buildings in general, and hangars in particular, bearing in mind the steep angles of attack which German dive bombers are capable of achieving.
(c) Aircraft should be widely dispersed, and as far away from hangars as possible, and never be permitted to congregate on the tarmac.
(d) Aircraft loaded with bombs should never be allowed in the vicinity of the tarmac and hangars.
(e) If the primary object of our fighters is to attack and destroy the enemy bombers, they should always guard against being wholly drawn off by enemy fighter escorts.

Prepared and circulated by the Deputy Directorate of Air Tactics August 27th, 1940. S.5539.

A German pilot prepares to embark on a combat sortie.

From 'Fighter Tactics' (1940)
AIR 16/274

10. <u>Fighter Tactics.</u>

It has been suggested that the only sound tactical method for a fighter to adopt is an approach, out of the direct line of fire of the defending gunners, as directly and rapidly as possible to *decisive* range, there to assume the most favourable firing position relative to the target and deliver a bullet group of sufficient size to cover the probable aiming errors and wander of aim. Decisive range will depend on the number of guns, their alignment, and the rate of fire. With two slow firing guns ranges over 100 yards were rarely decisive. Modern multiplication of guns, in the absence of a considerable advance in sighting technique, will not greatly increase the range at which fire will be consistently decisive, and has been offset by increases in speed and the consequent increased effect of moderate avoiding action. Even with eight guns fire is unlikely to be effective until the fighter is within 400 yards. The French officer interviewed could give little information regarding the combat in which the Messerschmitts were brought down, and seemed very reluctant to respond to tentative enquiries about the French pilot concerned. He did say however that the French pilot had attacked from above and behind and a little to port from short range (about 200m). The German was apparently completely surprised. The Messerschmitt 109 is at present fitted with four guns, whose rate of fire is comparable to that of the Browning, and all indications from combats reported hitherto, the Wellingtons in the Heligoland Bight, the Battles in France, and French experience point to the conclusion that German pilots try to approach on a curved path directly to a range of about 200 yds. above or below, thus supporting the above contentions. There is therefore, up to the present, little of nothing to add to the tactics laid down for our eight gun fighters except to emphasise the importance of reaching decisive range as rapidly and as much out of the direct line of fire as possible. The French Attache de Force Aerienne at 5 Corps H.Q. said that the German fighters invariably seemed to attempt to reach 200 yds. range on a curved path before opening fire. This experience, like our own, was based on very few combats, but seemed consistent.

11. <u>Bomber Tactics.</u>

Definite conclusions drawn from such limited experience for the guidance of our own bombers are clearly impossible, but it seems that the Messerschmitt 109 is unlikely to be effective much outside 200 yds. range. By vigilance and accurate fire gunners should therefore endeavour to start hitting before it reaches that range. Aids to such accurate shooting of urgent importance are:–

(i) A comparable volume of fire from turrets i.e. two to four guns augmented by cross fire from aircraft in good formation.

(ii) The provision and intelligent use of tracer in the manner suggested by Professor Malvill-Jones.

As an addendum it is suggested that straggling formations, lack of vigilance, and the beginning of rotating or corkscrewing manoeuvres at too early or too late a stage in the combat, will immensely increase the chances of the Messerschmitt 109 reaching a range at which its fire will be effective.

From 'Tactics for Fighters v German Formations' (1940)

Note on Enclos. 1A – TACTICS FOR FIGHTERS v GERMAN FORMATIONS.

A. There are one or two paragraphs which I would like to qualify:

1. [. . .] our success in combats over this country have not been so marked as the draft suggests. Enemy aircraft destroyed per fighter in May and June were 2.4 and from August 8th to October 9th. – 3.

2. [. . .] fighters with bombs, far from being an exception, have in the last fortnight become the rule. Confirmation has now been received that Me.109 drop their bombs flying straight and level at 20,000 feet.

3. [. . .] armament and armour on enemy aircraft have, within certain variations, been standard since the beginning of August, with the exception of Me.110 which has been armoured since that date against head-on attacks.

4. [. . .] I do not think the fighter escort can form a defensive circle and still continue to act as an escort to bombers; surely these must be alternatives.

5. [. . .] it is not quite clear how a fighter can remain on the defensive when the enemy are sighted.

B. There are two points hardly touched which seem to me to be important:

1. There has been a steady tendency to increase height in all types. Our fighters now frequently patrol at 30,000 feet and above. Advantage of height is often the decisive factor. As aircraft move more quickly in the horizontal plane than upwards in the vertical plane, errors of plotting in the latter plane are more difficult to correct.

2. Intercepts have shown that the enemy is constantly listening to our R/T transmissions and passing information back to their aircraft in regard to position and height of our fighters. I do not know how far Controllers realise that every word they say is listened to by the enemy. I would like to suggest that instead of giving height as Angels followed by a number, a method which can now only be regarded as a convenience of expression and not a code – height could be given as plus or minus a known zero. Zero could be varied as required by arrangement between

Sector Controller and Squadron Commander; e.g. if zero were 15,000, +5 would mean 20,000.

3. The G.A.F. have made a close study of day bombing, which, at all events before the war, they considered to be more important than night bombing because it offered a better chance of destroying the target.

They reckoned to do this by –

(i) Surprise
(ii) Dive-bombing attacks
(iii) Low-flying attacks
(iv) High-level bombing with escort

<u>Surprise</u> has proved impossible against this country.

<u>Dive-bombing</u> by Ju.87 was very expensive and Ju.88 seems to have proved difficult to pull out of dive, and so has not recently been used in this form of attack.

<u>Low-level attack.</u> Besides a large number by single aircraft, one very well executed attack was carried out against Kenley and a number against coastal aerodromes such as Manston and Hawkinge. Some, but not all of these proved expensive. On the whole this attack has been surprisingly little used.

<u>High level attacks</u> have been most extensively used and have, on the whole been more successful and less expensive.

A German fighter pilot explains dogfighting tactics to a subordinate.

C. There appear to be one or two Developments of their early technique:

1. The first escorts were too far from the bombers to prevent our fighters attacking: accordingly, as is shown in the draft memorandum, fighters now fly, not only immediately behind bombers, but also to one side, usually up sun and even in front, with generally two layers of fighters above.

2. They have used the sensitiveness of our reporting system to divert our effort from the main attack by sending numerous diversions to a variety of other points. This is probably the most difficult problem now confronting our reporting system.

   We have tried to meet this by –

   (a) Listening to their R/T and distinguishing bomber and fighter formations by D/F: this does not seem to have been very successful.
   (b) High flying reconnaissance aircraft: this experiment has not yet had a full trial.

3. The enemy have repeatedly, with negligible success, tried to catch our fighters on the ground by sending successive attacks fifty to sixty minutes after each other. On one occasion at least, this enabled the wing leader, owing to the particular circumstances in which he found himself, to order the Spitfires to attack the bombers while the Hurricanes took on the fighters.

Secondly, 12 Group have invariably concentrated the wing formation before moving into attack; 11 Group, no doubt from the necessity of circumstances, have frequently endeavoured to concentrate their squadrons across the path of advancing enemy formations. Sometimes contact has not been established between our squadrons, and it has often proved difficult to co-ordinate our attack.

It is difficult to compare accurately the results of wing formations with those of single squadrons because our information is so meagre, but in general, our casualties seem to have been lighter when a wing has gone into action. Moreover, one squadron has frequently proved insufficient to divert a determined attack from its objective.

October 14th, 1940.

From 'Fighters versus Fighters' (1940)

FIGHTERS VERSUS FIGHTERS:

It is probable that the enemy will operation independent fighter formations over this country for the purpose of:–

  (i) Gaining air superiority.
 (ii) Carrying out low attacks on aerodromes and dispersed aircraft.
(iii) Attempting to draw off our fighters prior to bombing attacks whilst our fighters are re-fuelling and re-arming. (This latter practice has been frequently carried out in France.)

The allocation of forces will be decided by the Group or Sector Commander, but Fighter Units should always remember that to waste petrol and ammunition under these circumstances may well be playing into the hands of the enemy. It may be necessary, therefore, for our fighters to adopt a purely defensive role for the protection of the aerodrome, and not to attack these fighters, who are in the nature of a decoy, so that when the bombing forces arrive they will be able to attack them and shoot them down.

When battle is engaged with fighters, a dog-fight nearly always ensues. It may then be a matter of individual combat, but whenever possible fighters should remain together so that they may afford mutual support.

When a fighter unit is attacking enemy fighters, Sections should be led into the attack together. As already stated, such attacks must invariably develop into a series of dog-fights and whenever possible our fighters should attempt to remain loosely in Section formation, or at least in pairs, so as to afford mutual support and to assist in the reformation of the unit after combat. On no account should individual fighters leave a formation to deliver attacks unless specifically ordered to do so.

A Polish fighter pilot poses by the side of his battle-damaged Spitfire.

SUMMARY:

The following points are again emphasised:–

(i) It is essential that leaders should weight up the situation as a whole before delivering attacks. Rushing blindly in to attack an enemy may have disastrous results, and will certainly be less effective

(ii) Never fly straight, either in the formation as a whole or individually. When over enemy territory alter course and height with a view to misleading A.A.

(iii) Keep a constant watch to the rear of the formation of aircraft.

(iv) Upon hearing close gun fire, turn immediately. Hesitancy in so doing may result in effective enemy fire. Do not dive straight away.

(v) Before taking off, search the sky for enemy fighters, and if they are known to be about turn as soon as possible after taking off. Enemy fighters have frequently dived on aircraft whilst taking off from their aerodromes. Similar remarks apply during approach and landing.

(vi) Conserve ammunition as much as possible. A short burst at effective range is usually decisive, and leaves further ammunition for further attacks.

(vii) Exploit surprise to the utmost. The enemy has been taught to do this, and you should be prepared accordingly.

(viii) Always remember that your objective is the ENEMY BOMBER.

Air Chief Marshal, Air Officer Commander-in-Chief,
FIGHTER COMMAND.

FG/S.18033/Ops.1.
29.5.40.

The following two documents relate to the sighting, configuration and the firing technique applied to RAF fighter armament. During the Battle of the Britain, both the Spitfire and the Hurricane were armed with eight belt-fed .303in (7.7mm) Browning guns, four in each wing. Each gun could fire 20 rounds per second, with enough ammunition for 16 seconds' total firing. All eight guns had to be 'harmonised' — i.e. set so that the fire from all guns converged at a single point at a set distance in front of the aircraft, the subject of discussion below. Although the eight machine guns could certainly deliver a heavy volume of lead, the non-explosive nature of the rounds meant that kills could be hard to achieve even after considerable numbers of rounds hit the target. The Germans invested far more in equipping their Bf 109 fighters with 20mm cannon; although these had far fewer rounds per gun than the British weapons, combined with machine-gun armament they had far more aircraft-wrecking potency. Cannon weapons gradually became part of Spitfire and Hurricane armament from 1941.

From 'Fighter Command Tactical Memorandum No. 5' (1939)

<u>FC/S.18033.</u>

> HEADQUARTERS, FIGHTER COMMAND,
> ROYAL AIR FORCE,
> BENTLEY PRIORY,
> STANMORE, MIDDLESEX.

> 26th November, 1939.

FIGHTER COMMAND TACTICAL MEMORANDUM NO.5.

FIRING METHODS IN AIR COMBAT.

1. A Study of Combat Reports has revealed a tendency to fire guns of 8-gun Fighters in short bursts.

2. This practice is uneconomical in ammunition and likely to lead to indecisive results.

3. Every time fire is opened from an 8-gun Fighter the nose is depressed and the line of sight is thrown off the target. If fire is then stopped and the sights re-aligned, they will again be thrown off the target as soon as fire is reopened.

4. Pilots must be prepared for this phenomenon and bring back their sights on to the target without ceasing fire; thereafter holding their sights on the target as long as the enemy permits them to do so.

5. Alternatively the sights should be aligned above the target before opening fire so that the alteration to the thrust line brings them on to the target.

6. With training and experience it may be possible to open fire with the sights on the target and to anticipate the drop of the nose by a backward motion of the control lever.

7. Pilots must pay particular attention to this point when firing their guns for practice over the sea. A cloud, or some other definite mark, should be taken as the point of aim, and efforts should be made to open fire with as little deviation as possible from the target.

Air Chief Marshal, Air Officer Commanding-in-Chief, Fighter Command, Royal Air Force.

Four of the eight .303in Browning machine guns, in one wing of a Spitfire.

From 'Fighter Command Tactical Memorandum No.7' (1940)

At a recent meeting of the Gun Sub-Committee the question of the harmonisation of 8-gun Fighters was discussed.

2. Although good results have been obtained with the Fighter Command method of horizontal dispersion, it was the consensus of opinion that more rapid and immediate effect might be attained if complete concentration on a point at 250 yards range were effected.

3. The enemy's attacks are so spasmodic and discontinuous that it is difficult to carry out trials of different harmonisations simultaneously.

4. I have therefore decided to order the complete concentration of all guns in 8-gun Fighters on a point at a range of 250 yards.

5. There is nothing final about this decision, and it is quite possible that, after a period of trial, I may decide to revert to the standard Fighter Command, or to some other system of harmonisation; but while this system of concentration on a point is in force, tactical methods now in existence must be slightly modified.

6. Experience has shown that the most vulnerable part of the Heinkel is the back of the engine, and it must be the object of every Fighter pilot who is using this

system to endeavour to obtain a concentrated burst of fire on the back of each engine separately.

7. Complete concentration will, of course, only be obtained at the exact range of 250 yards and, therefore, the bulk of the fire should be delivered as nearly as possible at that range.

8. This means that fire should normally be opened at about 300 yards, and that the overtaking speed should be kept low.

9. It will, of course, often happen that the pilot is unable to attain the desired range, but must open fire at longer range before the enemy disappears into a cloud.

10. The system now ordained may, nevertheless, give quite effective results at ranges up to 500 yards. It will be necessary, however, to exercise particular care in the matter of elevation, since there will now be no vertical dispersion of the pattern.

11. These orders do not preclude aim being taken at the fuselage if return fire is being experienced; but, as stated above, the main objective should be the back of each engine in turn.

Air Chief Marshal, Air Officer Commanding-in-Chief, Fighter Command.
FC/S.18033/Air.
23rd February, 1940.

A Hawker Hurricane tips down its nose and begins a fast dive.

A bitter tactical debate raged in the heart of Fighter Command in August and September 1940, one that established unhelpful rivalries in the RAF hierarchy. The two fighter Groups that did the lion's share of fighting during the Battle of Britain were No. 11 Group, headed by Air Vice-Marshal Keith Park, which covered the south-east of England and London, and No. 12 Group under Air Vice-Marshal Trafford Leigh-Mallory, assigned to cover East Anglia and the Midlands. No. 12 Group tended to act in a support role to No. 11 Group, the former scrambling to provide reinforcements for the latter when No. 11 Group became overstretched, which was often.

To set the context for the argument between Park and Leigh-Mallory, RAF fighters tended to be scrambled in squadrons, which typically consisted of 9–12 aircraft. These relatively small units would go up to face *Luftflotten* of 30–40 aircraft (mixed fighters and bombers), meaning that they were consistently outnumbered. The advantage of the squadron scramble, however, was that it was a relatively quick process to get the aircraft into the air, coordinated and vectored onto the target.

Leigh-Mallory did not regard the squadron action, or at least Park's expression of it, too favourably. He argued that Park's hit-and-run tactics, necessitated by the small squadron size, did not carry sufficient combat impact. To do more serious damage to the incoming German air units, larger numbers of aircraft needed to meet them in the aerial battlespace. To this end, he advocated the 'Big Wing', also known as the 'Balbo'. His idea was to get no fewer than 3–5 squadrons (as many as 60 aircraft) in the air together at one time, to make a mass coordinated attack that shattered the enemy force. He soon found fellow believers, one of the most prominent being Douglas Bader, the commander of 242 Squadron, who brought his squadron down to RAF Duxford to join other units there and form the 'Duxford Wing'.

The argument about Big Wing vs Squadron tactics grew incredibly bitter, with Leigh-Mallory and Bader on one side, and Park and Dowding on the other. As it happened, Park was not implacably opposed to the Big Wing principle, which he had himself used during the air battles over Dunkirk. Nor was there an ultimate winner in the argument, as the Big Wing tactic was never entirely tested to satisfaction. When it was attempted, Park's concerns that it would be too cumbersome and slow to organise seemed to be borne out. Regardless of the outcome, however, the debate illustrates how personalities as much as dispassionate analysis played their part in the Battle of Britain.

From 'No.12 Group Operation Instruction no. Reinforcement of No.11 Group' (1940)
AIR 16 375

NO.12 GROUP OPERATION INSTRUCTION NO. REINFORCEMENT OF NO.11 GROUP

December, 1940.

INFORMATION.

1. No.12 Group may be required to reinforce No.11 Group under certain circumstances, e.g.:–

(i) When enemy attacks are so strong or repeated so as to test the capacity of No.11 Group's resources.

(ii) When enemy attacks are directed north of the Thames and are accompanied by other attacks elsewhere in No.11 Group area.

(iii) When special opportunity exists for the surprise and destruction of enemy formations.

(iv) For guarding No.11 Group aerodromes when large sweep raids over France are employed by No.11 Group.

(v) When sweep raids by No.11 Group are being followed home by enemy fighting formations and bomber formations, for the purpose of shaking off any enemy formations.

INTENTION.

2. To provide a reinforcement up to wing strength to operate in No.11 Group area when circumstances demand this.

EXECUTION.

3. The wing formation will be employed on patrol lines as agreed between Nos.11 and 12 Group Headquarters.

4. Requests by No.11 Group for reinforcement will go direct to No.12 Group Controller and will state the task, minimum strength, time and line to be patrolled. The tactical methods to be employed by No.12 Group to remain a matter for No.12 Group decision.

5. Requests for reinforcements will be made with the maximum possible notice, and will be preceded by a preliminary warning whenever the necessity for assistance appears to be probable.

6. All day squadrons in No.12 Group equipped with V.H.F. are to be trained and should be ready to operate as a component of a wing formation for the reinforcement of No.11 Group. Night flying Squadrons and Squadrons fitted with H.F. will not be required for reinforcing purposes.

7. For the present the wing earmarked for reinforcement purposes will consist of [up to] three Squadrons and will be concentrated either at WITTERING or DUXFORD. Then COLTISHALL has been equipped with V.H.F. facilities, the wing may be ordered to concentrate there. Full use is to be made of Satellite aerodromes and normally not more than two Squadrons should be on one aerodrome.

8. The strength of the reinforcing formation to be employed will be decided by pre-arrangement in conjunction with No.11 Group.

9. Squadrons will be details to stand-by for reinforcement duties daily by this Headquarters.

10. Normally in fine weather when the enemy is active, the wing will be at AVAILABLE (15 minutes' notice) and No.12 Group Controller will advise No.11 Group Controller daily at 1000 hours what state it is maintaining. Any greater strength or higher state of Readiness required will be asked for by No.11 Group Controller. No.12 Group Controller will warn No.11 Group if a lower state of Readiness has been enforced by weather or other conditions.

11. As soon as preliminary warning of a request for reinforcement has been received, the appropriate Squadrons will be brought to "Readiness" by the Group Controller. As soon as this preliminary warning has been confirmed by receipt of a definite request, the appropriate wing formation will be ordered to take off.

An artwork of the Supermarine Spitfire, clearly showing its large elliptical wing area.

CONTROL.

12. The wing, from whichever base it operation, is to be controlled by DUXFORD as soon as it is in R/T touch with that Station when operating to the North of the Thames Estuary, and by HORNCHURCH as soon as it is in R/T touch with that Station when operating to the South of the Thames Estuary.

INTER-COMMUNICATION.

13. Arrangements have been made for all available R.D.F. information down to the latitude of DUNGENESS – GRIS NEZ to be told to No.12 Group.

14. Arrangements have also been made for DUXFORD to be put on the BROMLEY and MAIDSTONE Observer Centre teleprinter circuits as soon as lines can be made available. In the meantime BROMLEY will tell to COLCHESTER all plots in the BROMLEY areas north of the Thames, for re-transmission to DUXFORD.

15. No.11 Group will tell No.12 Group all other necessary information from Observer Corps and R.D.F. sources in respect of raids with which the wing may be required to deal.

16. To enable DUXFORD to control the fixer service of the wing formation, it will be necessary for all V.H.F. Squadrons to have one of the DUXFORD's Fixer Frequency Crystals of 6512.5 kes. in one aircraft of each Squadron. Squadron Commanders are responsible for ensuring that one of their aircraft is equipped with DUXFORD's Fixer Crystal before taking off to form the wing.

17. All Squadrons in the wing will receive the Pip Squeak Zero from DUXFORD Controller, but the leading Squadron only will be ordered to switch Pip Squeak in.

18. All R/T communication with the wing will be carried out on the Group Guard Frequency (6575 kes) which is fitted in channel "B" of all day flying V.H.F. aircraft.

19. Two crystals of HORNCHURCH fixer frequency (6412.5 kes) have been forwarded to every sector in the Group, and one is to be fitted in an aircraft of every squadron taking part in the wing formation. This can most easily be carried out by fitting the HORNCHURCH crystals in spare serviceable TR.1133's which can then be installed in any aircraft as ordered by the Squadron Commander.

20. When the wing enters No.11 Group area, the leader will call HORNCHURCH and ask for zero. This zero will be taken by all aircraft fitted with HORNCHURCH Fixer Crystals and this aircraft in the leading Squadron will switch Pip Squeak "in". Should this aircraft become a casualty the aircraft having the HORNCHURCH crystal in the second squadron will switch Pip Squeak "in".

21. When operation south of the Thames or if difficulty is experienced in working with DUXFORD when in the HORNCHURCH area, the Wing Leader will call HORNCHURCH and ask them to take over control. When this has been done, he will inform DUXFORD who will maintain R/T silence on the Wing Frequency except in an emergency. A similar procedure will be adopted when returning. HORNCHURCH will then maintain R/T silence on the Wing Frequency as soon as the Wing has been taken over by DUXFORD.

From 'Use of Wing Formations against Present Enemy Tactics' (1940)

SECRET

From:–   Headquarters No.11 Group
To:–   Officer Commanding, R.A.F. Station:

DEBDEN	NORTH WEALD	HORNCHURCH
NORTHOLT	TANGMERE	KENLEY
BIGGIN HILL		

Ref:–   11G/486
Date:–   15th October, 1940.

Use of Wing Formations Against Present Enemy Tactics

The use of Wings of two or three Squadrons is effective against enemy bombers with close fighter escorts for the following reasons:

(a) Much more warning from R.D.F. plots is received whilst the enemy bomber and fighter formations are assembling over the French coast; this gives the Group Controller plenty of time to order Squadrons up to operational height, in some cases well before the enemy raids commence to approach our coast;

(b) The bomber formations fly mostly between heights of 15,000 to 20,000 feet;

(c) Formations of enemy bombers and escorting fighters can be sent over to this country only in good weather conditions, which are suitable for interception by Wings.

2. Against the present enemy tactics, very high fighter patrols or raids, the use of Wing Formations has been found to have serious disadvantages for the following reasons:

(a) The warning received from R.D.F. plots is insufficient to place Squadrons at the required height in time to intercept the first wave of enemy fighters;

(b) The heights of enemy aircraft are much greater, thus requiring more time to intercept from above;

(c) The present enemy tactics are generally confined to days when considerable mist and cloud present.

3. Results have shown that Wings or pairs of Squadrons have only been successful in intercepting when there is a second or third wave of enemy fighters, and this can only be done if the Squadrons take off and climb independently to their operational height and then effect a rendezvous. When two or three Squadrons take off and climb together, the rate of ascent is found to be slower, thereby wasting valuable minutes during which time one or two Squadrons, operating singly, could attain position above the enemy fighter formations.

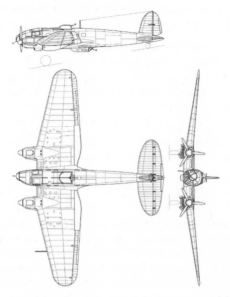

The Heinkel He 111 was the primary target for the RAF fighters.

4. The first wave of enemy fighter aircraft has usually been intercepted only by the Spitfire Squadron carrying out standing Readiness Patrol, and sometimes by one or two Spitfire Squadrons from Stand-by.

5. <u>Rigid</u> Squadron formations and Wing formations have been found to be ineffective against very high fighter raids for the following reasons:

(a) They can be broken up easily by attacks from above by small formations of enemy aircraft. Instances have occurred of even one or two enemy fighters having broken up a pair of our Squadrons;

(b) If enemy fighter aircraft happen to be below they can usually see a large formation of our fighters, and on account of their superior speed at high altitude they are able to withdraw before we can engage.

6. Enemy fighters have been coming over to this country at about 25,000 to 30,000 feet in fairly large numbers, and generally they have been spread out over a large area. Small formations up to about seven in number appear to work together. These small formations are compact but very flexible. Provided the enemy has the advantage of height, numerical superiority or inferiority does not seem to bother him as he makes

his attack, and never does he allow himself to make the fatal mistake of staying down and fighting on our level. Dive and zoom in small sub-formations are greatly favoured.

7. During two recent occasions when flying over Kent, I have seen pairs of Hurricane, also Spitfire, Squadrons, climbing in close company in rigid squadron formation, "section line astern", almost directly below enemy fighter formations; the enemy being disposed in small, flexible formations, flying within supporting distance of one another. This appeared to be inviting attack from above, and no action by Group or Sector controllers can protect our Squadrons in such circumstances.

8. On several occasions recently when one of our Squadrons has encountered enemy fighters below, the following obvious mistakes have been made:–

(a) A Squadron was ordered to break up and carry out individual attacks on superior numbers, resulting in a dog-fight, when the Squadron's task was, by repeated attacks from above, to engage the enemy fighter screen to protect other fighter squadrons climbing up from ground level to rendezvous.

(b) The whole Squadron has dived to attack simultaneously instead of keeping one or more Sections as above guard.

(c) When a small number of our fighters, after a general engagement, have found themselves above superior numbers of enemy fighters, they have failed to take advantage of their height, diving down and staying on the same level as the enemy fighters, instead of breaking up the enemy formation by dive and zoom tactics.

9. To deal successfully with the present enemy tactics it is necessary to adjust our methods as follows:-

(1) Squadrons operate in three sections of four aircraft in loose weaving formation to prevent surprise from above. The sections of four should be trained to break away and work in pairs.

(2) When a wing of two or three squadrons is patrolling a given area or patrol line, the squadrons should be spaced 2,000 to 4,000 feet apart, instead of patrolling in a rigid mass. If the top squadron is attacked from above, it should endeavour to draw the enemy down across the bows of one of our squadrons.

10. The object of the present enemy tactics is to wear down and to reduce to a minimum the effectiveness of our fighter squadrons. The latest German Air Force Order of Battle shows that the enemy has at his disposal for operations against this country rather more fighter aircraft than we have. Interrogation of prisoners of war, however, has shown that the German fighter pilots have frequently been making two, and sometimes three sorties a day over this country. Prisoners of War are still of opinion that the Spitfire Mk. 1 is superior in performance to any German fighters. It has been realised for some time that the latest German fighters have a superiority in speed and climb over the Hurricane, and Headquarters, Fighter Command have

been pressing the highest in the land to get earliest delivery of Mark II Hurricanes, and later the Mark III Spitfire, both having the Merlin XX engine.

11. A disadvantage which our fighter pilots have not had to contend with has been the carrying of bombs some hundreds of miles into enemy territory as done daily by a proportion of the German fighter pilots. Moreover, the German pilots operating over our territory have not the great advantage of being kept constantly informed by R/T of the approximate strength, height and position of their opponents. From whatever angle the problem is examined, it is clearly evident that our pilots are operating with many advantages on their side, and the time has arrived when our fighter squadrons must adopt more flexible and cunningly aggressive tactics when fighting over our own territory.

12. Now that the Squadrons in Nos. 12, 13 and 14 Groups are gradually building up and once more becoming fit operationally it is hoped to relieve Squadrons in this Group after a period of between six to eight weeks in the line. This period naturally depends upon the intensity of air fighting among other factors.

13. This instruction has been prepared as a result of a very careful scrutiny by the Group Commander of dozens of recent patrol reports and combat reports from our twenty day fighter Squadrons. Observations of our Squadrons on patrol over Kent, and various discussions with Sector and Squadron Commandeers have also been taken into account before putting this brief instruction in writing.

RAF pilots sprint to their aircraft following a 'Scramble' order.

14. In May and June our fighter squadrons, with all the disadvantages of fighting over enemy territory, defeated the German Air Force in N.W. France. From July to August, our fighter squadrons decisively defeated the German dive bombers and their escorts. From mid-August until the end of September our squadrons again won a decisive victory, this time over the German long range bombers with their heavy, close escorts. The task of our squadrons is now to defeat a slightly superior fighter force working under all the disadvantages of long range patrols over enemy territory. The present situation, where formations of thirty to fifty German fighters can reach and bomb the capital of the Empire before being effectively attacked is no longer tolerable. I look to all Sector and Squadron Commanders to review immediately our present ideas of fighter tactics and to set about the Bosche fighters in the same aggressive spirit that defeated his bomber attacks by superior numbers.

15. Sectors are to ensure that each Squadron receives three copies of this instruction, which is also to be brought to the attention of Sector Controllers.

Air Vice-Marshal, commanding, No.11 Group, Royal Air Force

[. . .]

6. Quite apart from cloud interferences, the lack of time due to short warning of the approach of raids frequently renders it inadvisable to detail Wings of three Squadrons. Experience has shown that it takes much longer to despatch, assemble and climb to operating height, a Wing of three Squadrons than one of even two pairs of Squadrons. Frequently Wings of three Squadrons have been attacked by enemy fighters whilst still climbing or forming up over their Sector aerodromes. It has been found better to have even one strong Squadron of our fighters over the enemy than a Wing of three climbing up below them, in which attitude they are peculiarly vulnerable to attacks from above.

7. In clear weather when the enemy attack develops in two or three waves, there is often time for the Squadrons of Sectors on the flank of the attack, e.g., Debden, Northolt and Tangmere, to be despatched as Wings of three Squadrons to meet the third incoming wave or to sweep across and mop up the retreating enemy bombers and close escort. There is rarely time for London Sectors to get Wing formations up to the desired height before the enemy reaches important bombing targets, e.g., factories, docks, Sector aerodromes.

8. Until we have V.H.F. in all Squadrons, it is not practicable for three Squadrons in a Wing to work on a common R/T frequency; at least, that is the considered opinion of the majority of the Squadron and Sector Commanders. Pairs of Squadrons can and do work successfully on a common frequency whenever the State of Preparedness in a Sector permits. Here again some Squadron Commanders prefer to be on a separate R/T frequency in order to have better intercommunication within their Squadrons.

CONCLUSION:

9. As a result of five months intensive air fighting in No.11 Group, it is clear that Wings of three Squadrons are not the most suitable formations under many conditions of TIME and WEATHER. On the whole, Squadrons working in pairs have obtained better results in home defence, especially as our practice since July has been to detail two or more pairs of Squadrons to intercept raids in massed formation. However, when conditions are favourable, Squadrons will continue to be despatched in Wings of three, but the only person who can decide whether Wings or pairs of Squadrons should be despatched is the Group Controller. He has the complete picture of the enemy's movements on a wide front from Lowestoft to Bournemouth, and must quickly decide whether the time and cloud conditions are suitable for pairs of Wing formations. Squadrons must therefore continue to study and develop fighting tactics in Wings of three Squadrons, which will probably become more common in the Spring of 1941.

10. Two copies of this Note are to be distributed to each fighter Squadron, and one copy is to be ready by each Sector Controller.

Air Vice-Marshal, Commanding, No.11 Group, Royal Air Force.

From 'Air Staff Note on the Operation of Fighter Wings' (1940)

AIR STAFF NOTE ON THE OPERATION OF FIGHTER WINGS

1. It has become apparent that on some occasions our fighters have been meeting the enemy on unequal terms both as regards numbers and height. In order to overcome or reduce this disadvantage, fighters must be operated in tactical units large enough to deal effectively with enemy formations and these units must be so controlled that they encounter the enemy without tactical disadvantage.

2. It is the purpose of this note to examine the circumstances in which fighter units of more than single squadrons should be operated and to evolve general principles for their employment.

3. It would be well first to summarise the disadvantages under which our fighters have in some instances operated. These are briefly as follows:–

    (i) Numerical inferiority. Squadrons have been sent up singly or in pairs to meet large formations of bombers escorted by still larger formations of enemy fighters. The operations of these squadrons have not been effectively co-ordinated with the operations of other squadrons in the same group, and adjacent groups, with the result that fighters have operated independently and ineffectively.

    (ii) There have been few opportunities for fighter formation leaders to discuss or concert operations with the leaders of other fighter formations.

    (iii) Fighters are frequently told to patrol at a height which puts them at the mercy of high flying enemy fighters.

    (iv) Fighters are "vectored" towards enemy formations in such a way that by the time they reach the plan position of the enemy, they are below him.

    (v) The limitations of H.F. R.T. preclude the possibility of operating a number of squadrons on the same frequency.

4. Examination of these disadvantages leads us to recommend the adoption of the following principles for operating fighter formations larger than squadrons.

Fighter Wing.

5. The minimum fighter unit to meet large enemy formations should be a wing of 3 squadrons.

"Balbo".

6. When necessary, to secure superiority in numbers or to reduce inferiority as far as possible, a force of 2 fighter wings should be operated as a tactical unit. This tactical unit of 2 wings will be referred to in this paper as a "balbo".

Composition of a wing.

7. A wing should consist of 3 squadrons of the same type and if possible Mark of aircraft.

8. All squadrons of a wing should operate from the same aerodrome, or failing this, from aerodromes within 2 or 3 miles of each other.

Composition of a "balbo".

9. A balbo should be composed of 2 wings. One wing may be of one type of aircraft and the other wing may be of another. Wings composing of a balbo should be so disposed that the wing having the aircraft of higher performance is further back from the zone of operations.

Control of wing.

10. In order to ensure sympathetic and effective control of the wing, one of the squadron commanders from the squadrons composing the wing should supervise the controlling of the wing from the Sector Operations Room.

Control of a balbo.

11. The wings composing a balbo will come from different sectors. The control of each wing will be supervised by a squadron commander from the wing, but the group headquarters should detail one of the sectors to co-ordinate the operations of the 2 wings of the balbo. The D/F positions of both wings should be shown in the Operations Room of the controlling sector.

Variations in control necessitated by V.H.F or H.F. R/T.

12. V.H.F. facilitates the control of balbos, but if squadrons are fitted with H.F. it is considered that difficulties in inter-communication are outweighed by the advantages in meeting large enemy formations with large fighter formations.

Spitfires keep formation at altitude, ready for action.

Control of balbos with V.H.F. R/T.

13. All the squadrons in each wing should operate on sector frequency (Button "B") and would have to be controlled on this frequency. Inter-communication between wings in a balbo would be by means of the Command frequency through aircraft on watch on this frequency.

Control of balbos with H.F. R/T.

14. Squadrons should operate on their squadron frequency; inter-communication between squadrons by R/T is impracticable except through ground stations. It will frequently happen when using H.F. that balbos will pass out of R.T. range of their sectors. When this happens it may be confidently expected that weather will be such that large enemy formations will be clearly visible from a distance, and vectoring, therefore, will be unnecessary.

15. The control of balbos operating at a distance from their controlling sectors even with V.H.F. is complicated by the sectors not having operations tables big enough to show the whole area over which balbos may have to fight. It is recommended that smaller scale "balbo tables" should be provided to show the tracks of enemy formations of more than say 50 aircraft. These tables should be small-scale replicas of the Fighter Command table, (say 10 miles to 1"). Consideration would have to be given to the method by which this information might be passed to sectors.

Units of wings.

16. "Esprit de wing" and consequent operation efficiency would be fostered by regarding wings as units and moving them complete from one station to another when rest or reinforcement is necessary, but this is obviously impracticable at present. It would be difficult to engender in a balbo the same spirit of unity which should inform a wing, but much could be done to promote good co-operation by encouraging personal contact between the pilots and particularly the leaders of the squadrons concerned.

Location of wings.

17. Wings should be located at stations from which they gain advantage in height over the enemy before they meet him, without having to turn. This may be impracticable except in special cases.

Group combined tactical plan.

18. The tactical plan on which the primary group should work ought to be based on the principle that although the aim is to destroy enemy bombers, the enemy fighters must be contained to enable bombers to be destroyed.

Role of wings.

19. The wing with the higher performance aircraft should take on enemy fighters. The wing with the lower performance aircraft should take on bombers, if any.

20. If the strength of enemy formations is low enough to warrant the use of only one wing, the wing leader should use his judgement in deciding what proportion of his force to devote to containing enemy fighters.

14.10.40

The two great RAF fighter aircraft that defined the Battle of Britain were the Supermarine Spitfire and the Hawker Hurricane. The Spitfire is the more famous and glamorous of the two, designed by R.J. Mitchell in the mid 1930s. With a high top speed, graceful lines and large elliptical wings that gave it outstanding manoeuvrability, the Spitfire was a near-perfect combat fighter, more than capable of dogfighting with the Bf 109s. Yet the fact remains that the Hurricane – heavier in profile and slightly slower than both the Spitfire and the Bf 109 – could turn tighter than its sleeker cousin and rival and provided a steadier gun platform. Combined with its use in larger numbers than the Spitfire, these qualities meant that the Hurricane actually accounted for 60 per cent of German air losses during the Battle of Britain.

From *Pilot's Notes: Spitfire IIA and IIB Aeroplanes Merlin XII Engine* (1940)

GENERAL FLYING

14. This aeroplane is stable, and rock-steady in flight at high speed. The controls are not ideal, because it will be found that the aileron control becomes exceedingly heavy at high speed, while the elevator remains comparatively light and sensitive. Individual aeroplanes vary slightly, but in most cases care is needed in the use of the elevator control at high speed, to avoid sudden increases of load factor or "g". During a tight turn or loop in bumpy conditions, movements of the pilot's body due to bumps are liable to cause movement of the controls and so large and sudden fluctuations in "g". It is then advisable to press the elbow into the side to steady it. All normal flying should be done by aileron and elevator control, and it will reduce fatigue if the feet are taken off the rudder pedals, as rudder control is only required in certain aerobatics and to assist extra rapid increase of bank if desired. It is particularly important that the feet should be off the rudder when flying by instruments.

The cockpit of a captured German Messerschmitt Bf 109.

[...]

FLYING BY INSTRUMENTS

15. It has already been mentioned that this aeroplane can best be flown without use of rudder control, as perfect co-ordination of controls is thereby achieved automatically without the pilot's assistance, this is particularly important when flying by instruments, as the mental concentration required of the pilot is eliminated.

16. Instrument flying on this aeroplane is normal. If the atmosphere is very bumpy the toes may be used to steady the rudder, but not for steering, which must be done by aileron control. If the aeroplane has been subjected to rapid manoeuvres just before the need for flying by instruments, the artificial horizon [. . .] may take five or ten minutes to settle down and so the Directional Gyro must be used for keeping a straight course. If the pilot suddenly runs into bad weather and flying by instruments becomes necessary (for instance a cloud bank which cannot be avoided) and if he is uncertain of his direction he must use patience to allow the compass to settle down – fly absolutely straight for three or four minutes, if necessary, until the compass is quite steady, then set the Directional Gyro to its reading and then turn on to the correct course.

STALLING

17. Though the stall usually occurs at low speed, it must not be forgotten that it can happen at any speed if the stick can be brought back far enough to put the wings at stalling incidence. This is possible, on this aeroplane, owing to the partial instability in pitch mentioned in para. 14. At high speed the stall is extremely "rough", there is a violent shudder and clattering noise throughout the aeroplane, which tends to flick over laterally and unless the stick is put forward instantly, a rapid roll and spin results, which may severely strain or break the aeroplane. At minimum speed the stall is the same as on most aeroplanes of similar type, i.e. one wing drops sharply and the aeroplane spins if not prevented by use of controls. Note the following:–

(i) Stalling speed with flaps UP – 75 m.p.h. A.S.I.
    Stalling speed with flaps DOWN – 71 m.p.h. A.S.I.

(ii) Stalling should be practiced, at a safe height, by holding the aeroplane in level flight, engine off, gradually bringing the stick back until the stall takes place (see remarks in next para. 18).

SPINNING

18. Deliberate spinning is prohibited. If an accidental spin occurs, there is no difficulty in recovering, provided the standard method is correctly used, i.e. full opposite rudder (maintained until the spin stops) and stick slowly forward when recovery begins, the rotation first speeds up, as the nose goes down, for at least one turn. The nose then goes further down, and not until then does the spin stop. About 2,000 ft. will be lost, so a margin of 5,000 to 6,000 ft. should be allowed, if possible. It is most important that no attempt is made to pull out of the dive too early. [. . .]

DIVING

21. The maximum permissible diving speed is 450 m.p.h. A.S.I. Note the following:–

(i) <u>Constant-speed airscrew</u>.– At maximum r.p.m. 3,000, the throttle must be 1/3 open. The pitch control need not be brought back to reduce r.p.m., the range of pitch is enough to hold down the r.p.m. at any airspeed.

(ii) The flaps must be up at over 120 m.p.h. A.S.I.

(iii) The aeroplane should be trimmed in the dive, i.e. the trimming tab control should be set to give no load on the elevator. This will lessen the possibility of excessive "g" being induced in easing out of the dive particularly if the pilot should release his hold on the stick owing to "blacking-out" or any other reasons. No difficulty in easing out of the dive will be experienced even if the aeroplane is trimmed in the dive as the elevator control is comparatively light and recovery from the dive is not resisted by excessive stability in pitch. Elevator tabs may be used, very carefully, as described in para. 14.

(iv) The rate of descent is very great, so ample height must be allowed for recovery.

AEROBATICS

22. <u>General remarks</u>.– The Spitfire is an exceptionally good aeroplane for aerobatics, but spinning is prohibited and aerobatics must not be performed below 5,000 ft. Aerobatics on this aeroplane may be done only by pilots who have adequate flying experiences of the aeroplane and who have written authority from their Squadron Commander. The Air Ministry and local regulations in force must be rigidly obeyed.

(i) <u>Trimming tabs</u>.– Complete trim can be obtained, (for flight "hands and feet off") by means of the top tabs, elevator and rudder. If lateral trim is out, the rudder tab can be used to counteract the turning affect. For example, if the pilot finds on attempting to fly straight hands off that the right wing goes down and the aeroplane turns to the right, he can adjust left rudder bias until the tendency to bank left counteracts the tendency to bank and turn right, and the aeroplane will then fly straight, though perhaps with the right wing slightly down. The elevator trimming tab is somewhat sensitive, and must be used slowly and carefully at all times (except at low speed in the extreme position). It may be used to assist manoeuvres and recovery from a dive, provided the pilot remembers the following points:–

(a) At high speed, rapid movement will strain the aeroplane.

(b) It relieves all loads on the elevator control, and the pilot must be careful not to continue winding it back (during a turn or loop, <u>however slowly</u>) beyond the point where the desired or safe tightness of turn, or load factor "g" is reached.

(c) If the pilot trims the aeroplane in a dive, he should keep his hand on the tab control, and use it, very gently, in recovery. Otherwise he might find it difficult to ease out of the dive, against nose heaviness.

(ii) <u>Slow-flying</u>.– Flying at low speeds, down to the stall, should be practised at a safe height, so that the pilot may become familiar with the feel of the controls. Feet should be kept on the rudder at low speed, as it might be needed if the aeroplane stalled.

(iii) <u>Stability in pitch</u>.– This aeroplane, though just stable in a dive, tends to be a little unstable in pitch (or fore-and-aft) during turns; as the turn is tightened up so the elevator control tends to become lighter, or, at least, fails to increase in weight to a desirable extent. Therefore, care must be used with this control, especially in rapid manoeuvres. When flying in busy conditions at high cruising speed, the pilot's body is bumped severely on the seat, and this is very uncomfortable, even for a short time.

23. <u>Characteristics and precautions</u>.– The chief characteristics of this aeroplane affecting aerobatics, and the preparations necessary are as follows:–

(i) High speed in the dive. This, coupled with the fact that the very effective elevator control, and comparative instability in pitch of this aeroplane, makes it very easy for the pilot to impose high load factors, or "g", when looping, doing tight turns, or pulling out of a dive. Although the safety factor of the aeroplane is about 10, it is well within the pilot's power to exceed "10g"; the wings would certainly fail if this figure is much exceeded. In very bumpy atmosphere, care is needed when manoeuvring with high "g", to prevent the arm from jerking the stick, owing to the jerking of the body in bumps, causing sudden fluctuations of "g", between about "2g" and "6g". A sudden upward bump bends the pilot's body and jerks the stick back, unless he jams his elbow against his body or the side of the cockpit.

(ii) Rapid loss of height in a dive. An ample margin of height must be allowed for diving either deliberately or if there is any chance of an accidental dive.

(iii) Great loss of height in the event of loss of control, such as a complete stall, flick roll, or spin. This is not only because of the rapid loss of height when stalled, or spinning, but also because of the need for gathering ample speed in the recovery dive, before beginning to ease out, owing to the fact that a semi-stalled condition of the wings persists well above stalling speed, and premature pulling out will cause another "flick", or a spin.

(iv) The high wing loading of the aeroplane. This is the chief cause of the characteristics already mentioned.

(v) Rather too effective elevator control and instability in pitch at large angles of attack (when turning or looping at high "g"). The results are already described in sub-para.(i).

(vi) Violent stall at high speed. Severe shudder and clatter is produced if the aeroplane is stalled at high speed (<u>see</u> para.17).

A British airman falls safely back to earth after a 'bail out'.

(vii) Great reserve of power.

(viii) Effective aileron control at all speeds down to the stall. It is, at the same time, excessively heavy at high speed. It should not be used with too much strength at very high speed, as it tends to twist the wings, which may already be under high torsional stress.

24. <u>General precautions</u>.– Note the following:–

(i) The pilot should ensure that the harness is tight enough, and be especially careful, for inverted flying, that it is not caught up in any way. This frequently happens, and causes the pilot's body to drop suddenly an inch or two, when the kink frees itself. This is most disconcerting.

(ii) See that the neighbouring sky, especially below, is clear of aircraft.

(iii) Do not use more power or higher r.p.m. than is necessary – on no account exceed the limits laid down. Many aerobatics, such as rolls, may be done at much less than full throttle. Cruising r.p.m. should be used (2,850) – if reduced below this, detonation might occur if the throttle is opened up to +9 lb./aq.in. boost, for any reason.

(iv) Use too high a speed rather than too low, especially when doing aerobatics on this aircraft for the first time, as there is then less likelihood of losing control, but handle the aeroplane correspondingly more carefully at the higher speeds.

(v) Do not continue any manoeuvre if vision fades owing to high "g", (see further remarks under Looping, para.25).

25. <u>Looping</u>.– This should be started at not less than about 300 m.p.h. A.S.I. When thoroughly proficient the pilot can do it at a slower speed, but there will then be a tendency to get too slow on the top, with a consequent likelihood of a flick-out or spin when the angle of attack is brought to stalling incidence if the stick is pulled back too far. Large loops may be started at any speed up to the maximum permissible, but the beginning of the loop must then be EXTREMELY GRADUAL, and the elbow pressed into the body or leg to prevent jerking of the over-sensitive elevator control in bumps. The method of looping is normal, (see Flying Training Manual, Chapter III). The pilot should endeavour to maintain constant "g", that is, to tighten up the start of the loop to about "3g", and then maintain this by very gradually continuing to tighten up the loop as speed decreases. The pilot has no way of telling the values of "g", but a rough guide is that the average pilot begins to lose vision at about "4½g", and so, if the loop is done well short of this "blacking out" point, it will be about "3g" or so. When loss of vision is approaching the pilot will experience a sensation of downward pull behind the eyes and ears, and vision will begin to fade. No manoeuvres should be continued if sight is lost, as the pilot loses one of his guides to the rate of loop, and might increase "g" to the point where the brain fails altogether or the wings break.

Note the following:–

(i) The elevator trimming tab may be used, either in the loop or in the recovery from the dive, but, if so, great care must be taken to move it slowly and not to continue moving it back beyond the point giving about "3g". Remember too, that if a vertical dive is started at a slow speed with the tab control too far back, (for example, if the speed gets too slow on the top of the loop, and the aeroplane is allowed to fall into a dive without "flicking-out"), the "g", or load factor, will rapidly become excessive as the aeroplane gathers speed.

(ii) The Rocket Loop, Large Loop, and other variations may also be done effectively.

(iii) The following example of the airspeed at various stages of a typical loop may be of interest:–

		Start	–	300 m.p.h. A.S.I.
90°	–	Vertical	–	200 m.p.h. A.S.I.
180°	–	Inverted	–	115 m.p.h. A.S.I.
360°	–	Level	–	290 m.p.h. A.S.I.

26. <u>Rolling</u>.– Rolling is very easy, though the aileron control is extremely heavy at high speed. It may even be done with feet off the rudder pedals, if it is "barrelled" a little, that is, a <u>slight</u> amount of positive pitch (or loop) maintained during the roll. Rolling is done in the normal way, as described in the Flying Training Manual, Chapter III. A roll may be either moderately slow, slow, or barrel, ("slow" refers to the rate of roll, not airspeed). The moderately slow roll is the best, as the engine can be kept running normally throughout. It should be started at a speed of anything over about 160 m.p.h. A.S.I. Slower speed than this is possible, even down to 110 m.p.h., but at this extreme there is danger of stalling and spinning if the stick is pulled back at all. At higher speeds than 200 m.p.h. or so, aileron control becomes excessively heavy, and at 300 m.p.h. or over the roll should be done extremely slowly, by easing the nose up 30° or 40° above the horizon and then using only enough aileron control to roll slowly, avoiding the use of any considerable force. The best method, to keep the engine running, is to ease the nose up to about 20° or 30° above the horizon, and then start the roll at moderate rate by aileron control, assisted, if desired, by a little rudder at first; (this is unnecessary). As the aeroplane rolls on to its back it must be kept straight, and the nose allowed to come down very slightly, but <u>not below the horizon</u>. As the aeroplane rolls out, top rudder should be used to keep the nose up, aileron control used, as required, to steady the roll (that is, to check any tendency to roll out quickly) and the aeroplane kept straight so that the nose is pointing just above the horizon in the original direction after the roll. First attempts should be made with slight barrelling – the roll started with the nose about 30° up, and the nose allowed to come down <u>almost</u> on to the horizon when inverted, and, as the aeroplane rolls out, to come <u>slightly</u> round the horizon and then up a little as the aeroplane levels. When proficient, the pilot will be able to cut out this barrelling completely, keeping the nose straight, just above the horizon, throughout the role, the engines continuing to run. If the engine shows signs of beginning to fade, the stick should be brought back a little, almost imperceptibly.

27. <u>The true slow roll</u>.– This can be done, if high speed is used at the start, but the engine will cut when inverted. This is done in the normal way, the nose being kept pointing straight in a constant direction, except when the wings are vertical at the start and finish, when it should be raised a little by the top rudder, to prevent loss of height. If the engine is throttled back as the roll is started, it will be possible to get the engine going again earlier in the final stages of the roll.

28. <u>The barrel roll</u>.– This may be done with feet off the rudder, and is an exaggeration of the barrel type of moderate slow roll already described.

29. <u>A series of rolls</u>.– These can be done very easily on this aeroplane [. . .] They should be barrelled at first, the rate of roll being slowed down in the last quarter of each roll to regain speed lost when the nose was up; but when proficient, the pilot can do these with the nose up about 10° or so with very little barrelling.

30. <u>Climbing rolls and gliding rolls</u>.– These can also be done, the principles being the same. In doing gliding rolls, on a slightly down hill path, the pilot must be careful not to let the nose drop into a steep dive, and then pull out roughly. They are the most difficult type of roll to do properly.

31. <u>Upward roll</u>.– This is a useful exercise, but should not be overdone – on no account should the engine be over-revved; but speed at the start should be high, and the aeroplane eased up very gradually at first. When pointing vertically, rudder may be used to assist aileron, but not enough to deflect the nose appreciably. Do not hold the vertical attitude too long (watch the airspeed and start "recovery" while speed is still well over 100 m.p.h. A.S.I.). Otherwise a tail slide will result, which may break the control surfaces or connections, unless these are held rigidly central, which may be impossible. Finish off by cartwheeling and quarter rolling, or by allowing the nose to drop forward (not sharply enough to stop the engine), or by completing a loop to the inverted position and half-rolling out.

32. <u>Downward roll</u>.– This is useful in combat at the start of a vertical dive, before speed has become excessive. Rolls may be done equally well either to left or right, and pilots should practice this to avoid becoming "one-sided".

33. <u>Half roll off the top of the loop</u>.– The loop should be started with more speed than for a plain loop, and the roll begun directly the opposite horizon comes into view, as the pilot looks "up" through the dome of the hood, while the nose is still about 30° or 40° above the horizon. It should be regulated in such a way that the nose continues to come down gradually, as the aeroplane rolls out, until it is just above the horizon at the end. This will keep the engine running and ensure that the aircraft continues to gain height during the roll out. The aeroplane should then be travelling

A Spitfire cockpit, showing the machine-gun button on the circular joystick.

on exactly the opposite course to its original. This also may be done equally well to left or right. The pilot's weight should <u>not</u> come on to the shoulder strap at any time.

34. <u>Flick manoeuvres</u>.– The high-speed variety of flick-roll or flick half-roll must ON NO ACCOUNT be done. It is liable to cause severe strain, is clumsy and uncomfortable, and, being extremely easy, has no training or other value of any kind. But a flick-roll at low speed, and low r.p.m. done very gently, is a useful exercise in timing and control at low speeds, and prevention of spin. It is done by throttling well back, slowing down to about 140 m.p.h. A.S.I., and then very gently moving the stick back and, at the same time, applying rudder. The nose will rise and yaw, and, as the control angles are steadily increased, the aeroplane will suddenly start to "auto-rotate", or flick. If the stick is kept back the aircraft would then spin, but, as soon as the aeroplane approaches an even keel (at about the moment when the wings are vertical) the stick is put forward, and, as the flick ceases, the controls used to steady the aeroplane until the roll is completed. If this is done too late the aeroplane will continue to flick, until it does part of a turn of a spin; if done too soon the flick will stop, and the rest of the roll must be done by aileron control, in the normal way.

ON NO ACCOUNT CARRY OUT FLICK MANOEUVRES <u>EXCEPT AT LOW SPEEDS</u>, but remember that low speed makes spinning more likely if the controls are mishandled. Ample height should be allowed (<u>see</u> Stalling and Spinning, paras. 17 and 18). Other variations of loops, rolls and so on may be carried out.

35. <u>Inverted flying</u>.– This is normal. Ensure that the harness is tight, and follow each strap to its attachment to <u>ensure</u> that is has a straight "run" and is not doubled over or caught up. Keep the seat well down to avoid bumping the head. Do not use rudder control when turning inverted. It is best to half-roll into and out of the inverted position. If recovery is made in a half-loop, the elevator tab should be used, very carefully, as the aeroplane may tend to get nose heavy as it gathers speed. DO NOT trim with the tab when inverted, for this reason – keep the nose up by the necessary force on the elevator control, if the aeroplane is nose-heavy. Do not fly inverted unless provision is made to prevent fouling the engine and aircraft with oil or coolant. Watch oil pressure, and do not open up the engine again until oil pressure is restored.

COMBAT MANOEUVRES

36. Aerobatics, though vitally important as training for the mastery of the aeroplane, and for tactical manoeuvres, are not of the slightest use for such manoeuvre and combat, if carried out at <u>aerobatics</u>. That is to say, they are none of them used, because they are too slow, except one or two of the simplest when merged into simple, smooth and rapid changes of position.

37. In air fighting the pilot, when climbing or manoeuvring for position <u>before</u> the attack, must obtain the last ounce of performance from his aeroplane. Aerobatics are not the quickest way of getting from position A to position B in the air. When

actually attacking, the pilot concentrates on nothing else except bringing his guns to bear on the target. Therefore all his manoeuvres are simple turns, or a smooth combination of pitch and roll merged uniformly into one another. To give two examples:–

  (i) If the pilot wishes to attack an enemy aircraft passing 500 ft. overhead on an opposite course, he does <u>NOT</u> do a half-loop followed by a half-roll – it takes too long; he makes a quick, smooth, and absolutely uniform climbing turn in the best direction (not necessarily free from skidding, if this will help speed up the turn without loss of speed).

  (ii) Diving on to an enemy is done in the simplest and quickest way – by a swift and smooth roll, turn, cartwheel, dive and pull-out all merged into one – <u>NOT</u> by a complete half-roll followed by a quarter loop, and perhaps half a downward roll and pull-out, "by numbers" – it would take longer. <u>The simplest possible manoeuvre is the most efficient.</u>

38. <u>Turning circle</u>.– Never attempt a "tail-chase" with an enemy aeroplane having a smaller turning circle that the Spitfire. It is likely that most aircraft of lesser top speed [though it does not necessarily depend on that, but rather on stalling speed and other things] will be able to out-turn the Spitfire. Therefore the pilot should break off an attack the instant his gun-sights cease to "bear". It is not intended here to say more about fighter tactics, but this is a matter concerning the aerodynamic control of the aeroplane. If a turn of the smallest diameter, or at the quickest rate of change of direction <u>is</u> required at any time, the pilot must not tighten it up too closely to the stalling incidence. Even if the aeroplane does not begin to shudder or otherwise initiate an imminent stall, it may not be turning quite as quickly as it would if the stick is very slightly eased forward. If stalling incidence is reached, the aeroplane usually does a violent shudder, with a loud "clattering" noise, and comes out of the turn with a violent flick. This would be a serious loss of advantage in combat.

39. <u>Manoeuvrability</u>.– Manoeuvrability in combat consists of two separate and distinct features:–

  (i) Quickness of rate of change of direction, or rate of turn – and, secondary to this, smallness of turning circle (treated above). Very roughly speaking, this is a function of the stalling speed, – that is, an aeroplane with a high stalling speed has a large turning circle.

  (ii) Quickness of change of attitude – that is, shortness of time necessary to go from straight flight to vertical bank. Seconds may be gained at the beginning of a tail-chase by light and effective aileron control. An aeroplane cannot reach its best rate of turn until it is in a vertical bank (though bank must, of course, be reduced to less than the vertical if the turn is sustained for more than about 180°). The Spitfire is not good in this respect; its aileron control is very heavy at high speed (over 300 m.p.h.) and rudder should be used to assist rapid roll if necessary.

40. <u>Blacking-out</u>.– Never increase the load factor, or "g", in tightening up a turn or loop, or pulling out of a dive, to such an extent that loss of vision (or "blacking out") occurs. It has several disadvantages:–

(i) It is dangerous, partly because it may lead to complete unconsciousness if "g" is further increased, and partly because the pilot loses all guides to the control of the aeroplane except his (often misleading) physical senses, and may either (supposing he is in a steep dive) fail to complete pulling out, and continue into the ground, or pull out too quickly, – quite easy to do owing to the rather over-effective elevator of the Spitfire, coupled with the aeroplane's comparative lack of stability in pitch, – this might result in complete unconsciousness or break-up of the aeroplane.

(ii) The pilot is immediately at a disadvantage. In combat he loses sight of the enemy, and at any time he cannot complete the manoeuvre efficiently.

<u>Note</u>.– Every pilot should practice subjecting himself to high "g", but <u>short</u> of the blacking-out point. This will increase his capacity to withstand it, and give him an advantage over an opponent who blacks-out at a lower "g" than he does.

CHAPTER 4
SUPPORT SERVICES

It was not only the aircrew of the RAF who found themselves in harm's way during the Battle of Britain. The Luftwaffe's policy of attacking RAF aerodromes also put ground crew directly in the line of fire; a total of 312 ground personnel were killed and 451 were wounded in these raids.

The fact was, the fighter pilots were purely the very visible tip of the operational iceberg, being supported from below by many thousands of personnel, men and women, in different professions, all of whom were essential to the working of the whole. The most obvious connection between the pilots and the rest of the RAF were those personnel responsible for aircraft repair and maintenance. Because of the priority to keep the aircraft operational, maintenance crews might work around the clock, often through the night, every night, to ensure that the squadron's aircraft would be fit to fight when the sun rose the next day. Fifteen-hour days could be the minimum.

Beyond the maintenance crews, however, there were a great host of other roles – meteorologists, logisticians, administrators, cooks and mess workers, engineers, radar operators, intelligence experts, administrators, postal workers, and more. Women made a pronounced contribution to this war effort, especially those belonging to the Women's Auxiliary Air Force (WAAF). They worked across the board in catering, meteorology, radar operation, wireless communications, aircraft maintenance, codebreaking, aerial photography analysis and as plotters in operations rooms. Without such myriad efforts, often conducted with little public acclamation, the aerial defence of the UK would not have been possible.

The text in this chapter, from the *Royal Air Force War Manual*, has at times a rather expeditionary feel, referring as much to operations overseas (the RAF did have many colonial outposts) as home defence. Yet even with this context, the document gives a deeper view into what elements made the RAF function in the round.

From *Royal Air Force War Manual, Part 2, Organization and Administration,* 2nd edition (1940)

CHAPTER VIII
THE SERVICES

[. . .]

The Meteorological Service

13. The meteorological service is responsible for:–

  (i) The supply to the policy staff of forecasts and data regarding the meteorological conditions at different times of the year in the theatre of war with a view to the planning of operations.
 (ii) The supply of meteorological data affecting the choice of aerodromes.
(iii) The issue to formations and units of accurate weather reports, forecasts and wind data for air operations.
 (iv) The issue of additional data; for example, warnings of sudden changes in wind or weather.
  (v) Forecasting for the information of the policy staff of conditions favourable for enemy air operations.

14. The head of the meteorological service is entitled the Chief Meteorological Officer.

15. The personnel of the meteorological service is supplied from R.A.F. sources. The service organization includes, in addition to the section at the senior formation headquarters, where forecasting will normally be carried out, sections at the headquarters of certain subordinate headquarters and sections at out-stations either with R.A.F. units or detached.

Survey Service

16. The survey service is responsible for:—

  (i) Making topographical, geological and trigonometrical surveys.
 (ii) Issuing the necessary technical information for railway, geological and all other surveys.
(iii) Distribution of maps and all air photographs to formations.

17. The survey service is one of the services which will be arranged or improvised in accordance with the circumstances of the campaign. The head of the service will be entitled the Chief Survey Officer. He is represented where necessary on the headquarters of lower formations.

The billiard room at an RAF training college.

Services Directed by Administrative Branch— Organization Section

General

18. The services directed by the organization section of the administrative branch of the policy staff are described below. The units which carry out the maintenance duties described in Chapter XV are directed administratively as a service. The status of the personnel of these maintenance units, however, is in no way affected; they are interchangeable, if necessary, with personnel of the fighting units.

19. The organization section is responsible for the direction of the following:—

   (i) Maintenance organization.
  (ii) Canteen service.
 (iii) Labour service.
 (iv) Postal and parcels forwarding service.
  (v) Printing and stationery service.
 (vi) Supplies service.
 (vii) Transport service.
(viii) Transportation service.
 (ix) Works service (including lands).

Also, so far as concerns stores accounting, the organization section directs the accounting service.

20. The extent to which the Army is responsible for provision of the above services when air forces and army forces are operating together is dealt with in Chapter X.

Maintenance Organization

21. The maintenance organization, which is operated jointly by the engineer and equipment services, is responsible for the establishment and operation of maintenance units of all kinds, for the supply and repair of aircraft, aero engines and motor transport, and all material for fighting purposes, such as armament and wireless apparatus; also material peculiar to the Royal Air Force, such as clothing of R.A.F. pattern.

22. At home this organization is grouped together in one command known as the Maintenance Command. The Maintenance Command, besides being responsible for maintenance at home, is also responsible for supplying those requirements of the overseas commands and of other air force formations operating outside the United Kingdom, which have to be sent to them from the United Kingdom.

23. The Maintenance Command includes a salvage organization for salving aircraft that crash in the United Kingdom in war.

24. In overseas commands and in the field the maintenance organization is composed of certain units whose duties are briefly described below.

(i) *Port Detachment.*

The duties of the port detachment are to arrange for and facilitate the clearance of R.A.F. material from the dock area. The establishment of the port detachment may be included in the aircraft depot but it will carry out its work independently.

(ii) *Aircraft Depot.*

This consists of a headquarters and appropriate sections, some of which may be detached. The depot holds and supplies stores for the force and collects them as necessary. Stores sufficient for three months' normal consumption are held. Repair sections carry out, up to the extent of their resources, repair and overhauls for the force which are beyond the capacity of the fighting units. The detachable sections may include salvage sections which will work in the forward area and whose duties are to collect aircraft and motor transport salvage and to send it for repair by the most suitable route.

The aircraft depot establishment is sufficiently flexible to enable advanced detachments to be sent forward into appropriate localities to carry out repair and overhaul work which, owing to the circumstances of the campaign, it may be inadvisable or uneconomical to send back to the depot in the base area. The aircraft depot is not a mobile unit. Aircraft depots in a campaign on a large scale may be completely sub-divided into stores depots and various types of repair, ammunition or fuel depots. Laundries and special workshops may also be required in these circumstances.

(iii) *Air Stores Park.*

This is normally a stores distributing and collecting unit and it is mobile. The park is equipped with transport which enables it to work normally over a radius of 25–40 miles. Sufficient stores are held to supply one month's normal consumption for a maximum of 5 or 6 squadrons. The number of air stores parks working in conjunction with an aircraft depot will depend upon both the distribution and the number of squadrons to be supplied. The location and administration of air stores parks are the responsibility of the commander of the formation which they serve. Their technical administration and replenishment are, however, the responsibility of the heads of the equipment and engineer services.

25. The personnel of the maintenance organization is provided for in R.A.F. establishments, and may include a large percentage of civilians.

Fitters at work on an RAF aero engine.

Canteen Service

26. The canteen service will be responsible for providing facilities in the theatre of war for the purchase by the troops of food, tobacco and other articles not provided free from air force funds.

27. The service will be organized as an adjunct to the supplies service. General supervision of the service will be exercised by the service staff at headquarters. The management and financial control however will be vested in the head of the canteen service, who will be an officer nominated by the Navy, Army and Air Force Institutes.

Labour Service

28. The duty of the labour service is to provide labour from sources other than units in the field in order that the latter may be able to devote themselves to the

greatest possible extent to their special duties of fighting, technical maintenance, and supply.

29. The special duties of the head of the labour service and his representatives are:—

(i) To investigate the requirements for labour in consultation with the policy staff and heads of the services or their representatives.

(ii) To allot labour units.

30. The officer and N.C.O. personnel of the labour service will be found from sources and in such manner as may be found expedient in the theatre of war. They will normally be drawn from personnel unsuitable to take their place in combatant units or specially qualified by a knowledge of languages or in other ways.

31. The rank and file of the corps will be drawn from the following sources: —

(i) Men enrolled on a civilian basis in the theatre of operations.

(ii) Men specially enlisted for the labour corps.

(iii) Other available sources, such as prisoners of war and men physically unfit for combatant duties.

32. The unit of the service is a labour company. So far as possible each company should be composed of men obtained from the same source, i.e., from one only of the three above mentioned.

33. Civilian units will consist of personnel hired in friendly or allied territory, or of personnel requisitioned in hostile territory. Hired personnel will be obtained in the open market either individually or through a local contractor, chief, or head man. Requisitioned labour is obtained through local authorities in accordance with the regulations for requisitioning in the theatre of war. The personnel of civilian labour units is governed by the rules for civilians laid down in Chapter XXI.

Postal and Parcels Forwarding Service

34. The postal and parcels forwarding service will be responsible for establishing and working a postal system for the carriage of official and private correspondence and Parcels in the theatre of operations. This service is for the benefit of the forces in the field, including foreign attaches and civilians employed by or accompanying the forces.

35. The source of the personnel of the service and the details of its organization will depend upon the nature of the campaign. When air forces and army forces are operating together, the postal and military forwarding services of the army will cater for the air forces in the theatre of war.

A wireless operator mechanics' workshop.

Printing and Stationery Service

36. The printing and stationery service is responsible for letterpress printing and for the supply of printed forms, books and stationery. The detailed arrangements for this service will depend on circumstances and cannot be stated in advance. (See Chapter X, para. 20.)

Supplies Service

37. The supplies service is responsible for the supply of food, fuel, petrol, oil, lighting material, disinfectants and medical comforts to the forces in the field.

38. The supplies service is usually combined with the transport service under a head of the combined service, who is represented at the supreme headquarters. The immediate subordinates of the head of the combined service belong severally to the supplies and to the transport services. The functions and control of the two services of supplies and of transport are separate throughout their organizations.

39. The basic principle of supply is that field units should have in advance of railhead and, independent of a breakdown of the lines of communication, two days' rations and one iron ration. These stocks are replenished by delivery at a point within reach of the consuming unit, of one day's supplies each day.

40. The service is responsible for the provision of this daily replenishment and for the organization of a supplies column, carrying supplies for several days for use in emergency when daily replenishment is impracticable.

41. In addition, the supplies service is responsible for the provision of supplies in depots, parks and dumps, including "detail issue stores" for the purpose of

issuing rations in detail to small parties or detachments in formation or lines of communication areas.

[. . .]

Transport Service

43. The transport service is responsible for the provision and upkeep of its own M.T., but not of M.T. belonging to units not in the transport service.

44. The head of the transport service is borne on the headquarters establishment but is normally one of the two immediate assistants of the head of the combined supply and transport service. (See para. 38 above.)

45. The operation of the supplies and transport system in connection with movement in the theatre of war is described in Chapter XVI.

Transportation Service

46. The transportation service is responsible for executive action in connection with the use of docks, railways, and inland water transport, and may be required to operate as well as control the working of these services in all respects. Coastwise sea transport by small vessels will also be the responsibility of the transportation service.

47. The head of the transportation service is borne on headquarters establishment and his subordinates are stationed at such points as the technical working of the service may demand.

48. The head of the transportation service will be responsible for co-ordinating the work of the following subordinate services, the whole or a part of which may be brought into being according to the conditions of the campaign:

   (i) Railways.
  (ii) Light railways.
 (iii) Docks.
 (iv) Inland water transport.

He is also responsible for the provision and custody of stores required for the transportation service and for the holding of transportation stores.

49. The transportation service, including its subordinate services, will be under the direct supervision and control of the movement section of the staff in the theatre of operations.

50. The responsibilities of the head of each of the subordinate transportation services will be executive in respect of the transport agency with which they are concerned.

51. For transportation arrangements when air forces and army forces are operating together, see Chapter X, para. 20.

Airmen at work in an engine repair shop.

Works Service

52. The works service is responsible for:—

(i) The purchase, requisition and hire of lands, aerodromes, training grounds, buildings, and billets, and for dealing with all claims made in connection therewith except such as may be dealt with by a Claims Commission, if one is established.

(ii) The construction of buildings, including store sheds, offices and workshop buildings; installations, including electric power stations, pumping stations with distributing mains, sanitary and fire protection systems, bakeries, laundries, baths and disinfecting stations.

(iii) The supply of prime movers for installations, except where provided by another administrative service.

(iv) Construction work necessary for the transportation service when the requisite transportation construction units are not provided.

(v) Construction and upkeep of roads and cemeteries.

(vi) Operation of electric power stations and pumping stations, except where undertaken by another administrative service.

(vii) Provision, local production, holding and despatching of engineer stores, both for works and field engineering and for camouflage.

53. The head of the works service is borne on the headquarters establishment. His representatives are not normally located at the headquarters of subordinate formations, the lands representatives (officers appointed by reason of special qualifications) are located in offices distributed throughout the theatre of war on a

territorial basis; other representatives are located as the work may require from time to time. Their duties are of a general administrative nature, with the exception of repair work and work in connection with the operation of machinery.

54. Except in circumstances of great emergency, which should be reported at once to superior authority, the inception of works services without reference to the responsible representative of the head of the service, is prohibited.

55. Works services for a R.A.F. contingent when operating with army forces are provided as described in Chapter X, paras. 27 and 28.

Services Directed by the Administrative Branch— Personnel Section

56. The following services are directed by the personnel branch of the policy staff:—

   (i) Chaplains service.
   (ii) Graves service.
  (iii) Medical service.
  (iv) Provost service.
   (v) Accounting service.
  (vi) Educational service.

Chaplains Service

57. The chaplains service is responsible for the spiritual and moral welfare of all personnel in the field.

58. The head of the service is the principal chaplain at command headquarters. His representatives in subordinate formations are shown in war establishments.

59. The personnel of the service is provided from the R.A.F. Chaplains Branch. The distribution of chaplains is effected, in the recognised religious denominations, by the principal chaplain and his representatives in formations. The number of chaplains attached to a formation headquarters will vary according to the number of units allotted to the formation.

60. Chaplains must work in close co-operation with the medical and graves services. The senior chaplains of formations are responsible for making the necessary arrangements to ensure that adequate provision is made for attendance on the wounded and dying and for officiating at the burial of the dead.

Graves Service

61. The Director-General of Graves Registration and Enquiries is responsible for arranging for the provision of suitable cemeteries, for ensuring the recording of all burials, and for providing means of identification of graves. In addition, the

graves service is also responsible for replying to enquiries, in respect of the burial of deceased personnel, made by relations or friends of the deceased.

62. The graves service is not responsible for the collection, searching and identification of the dead, the digging of graves or the carrying out of burials. These are the duties of the air force personnel themselves.

63. The head of the service at command headquarters will be a representative of the Director of Graves Registration and Enquiries.

64. The graves service will be organized in graves registration units. The units are distributed, if necessary, by detachments in locations varying from time to time. The personnel of the service will be arranged at the outset of a campaign from the most suitable source.

[. . .]

Armourers assembling aerial guns.

Medical Service

66. The medical service is responsible for advising commanders as to measures for the preservation of the health of the air forces, particularly the flying personnel, and the prevention of disease. It is responsible for the collection, professional care and treatment of sick and wounded in the theatre of operations, and their evacuation from it. It is also responsible for the local administration of medical units and, in conjunction with the appropriate branches of the policy staff, for their location. The service is charged, in addition, with the duty of the supply and replenishment of all medical equipment.

67. The head of the service at command headquarters is entitled the Principal Medical Officer. He is represented in subordinate formations. These representatives, in addition to performing their administrative duties, control the medical units and sections in their respective formations and areas.

68. The Principal Medical Officer is responsible for coordinating the work of the organizations dealing with:—

  (i) Medical and surgical treatment.
  (ii) Hygiene and sanitation.
  (iii) Dental surgery.
  (iv) Nursing.

These organizations are represented at command headquarters and in formations and areas as necessary for the technical working of the medical service as a whole.

69. The personnel of the medical service is found from R.A.F. sources; but under certain circumstances [. . .] the medical services in the field may be supplemented from army sources. Nursing duties for the R.A.F. Medical Service are performed by the Princess Mary's R.A.F. Nursing Service.

70. Units of the medical service are allotted to formations in accordance with the requirements of the situation. The actual distribution of these units is made by the commander on the recommendation of the Principal Medical Officer.

71. In the field the postings, promotion and replacement of all medical personnel, whether in medical units or borne on the establishment of non-medical units, are the responsibility of the Principal Medical Officer or his representatives, who will issue their orders concerning these matters through the personnel section of the policy staff.

[. . .]

An RAF medical school laboratory.

Provost Service

73. The provost service is responsible for:—

  (i) Assisting generally in the maintenance of discipline and ensuring compliance with regulations.

(ii) Assisting in the collection and disposal of stragglers and taking into custody and disposing of prisoners of war.

(iii) Arranging for the arrest of unauthorized persons found within the lines, all persons plundering, marauding, making unlawful requisitions, or committing offences of any kind.

(iv) Executive duties in connection with control of military and civil road traffic.

(v) Ensuring that due facilities for stating and proving their cases are given to inhabitants bringing complaints against R.A.F. or army personnel and for the protection of members of the forces against frivolous and unjust charges brought against them by inhabitants.

74. Where their duty brings them into contact with the civil population, personnel of the provost service work in close touch with the Field Security Police who are administered and controlled by the air branch of the policy staff as part of the intelligence organization.

75. The head of the service in the theatre of war is the Provost Marshal, and he is represented where necessary in subordinate formations. He commands the R.A.F. Police and is responsible for their organization, efficiency and general distribution. Command is exercised through the representative of the provost service in the formation concerned.

76. The personnel of the service is provided from R.A.F. or Army sources according to circumstances. The units are organized as:—

(i) Provost squadrons.
(ii) Provost companies.
(iii) Provost sections.

77. In emergency, the members of the provost service may call upon any R.A.F. or Army personnel to assist them in providing guards, sentries or patrols. All persons belonging to, or employed with, the forces in the field are required to give every assistance to the provost service in the execution of its duty.

Accounting Service

78. The accounting service in the field has responsibilities requiring direction by two sections of the administrative branch. For duties in connection with pay, it is directed by the personnel section. For duties in connection with stores accounting, it is directed by the organization section. The head of the service for convenience is directed by the commander through the S.O.A.

79. The accounting service is charged with the following pay duties:-

(i) Provision of funds, banking, currency and similar services.
(ii) Preparation of accounts. Issue of pay and allowances.

   (iii) Payment for services performed for the Royal Air Force.

   (iv) Accounting for cash expenditure and receipts.

   (v) Making claims against individuals or others for repayments and securing collection of the monies due.

   (vi) The administration of a central office for payment of requisitioning claims.

80. The degree to which stores accounting will be applied in the field must be decided in accordance with the circumstances of the campaign. In normal circumstances in a theatre of war stores accounting will probably be confined to maintenance units only. Such stores accounting as is carried out will be designed to assist the administrative branch of the staff and the maintenance organization in their administrative control of such matters as:—

   (i) Estimating expenditure and future requirements.

   (ii) Detection of weakness in organization and administration of stores.

   (iii) Fixing responsibility for appropriation of material to specific work and for custody of articles of equipment in use.

81. The head of the accounting service at command headquarters is entitled the Command Accountant. He is represented where necessary in lower formations.

82. The personnel of the service is provided from R.A.F. sources. Their distribution is effected by the commander as required, on the recommendation of the Command Accountant.

83. The system of stores accounting in the field is laid down in A.P. 830 Royal Air Force Equipment Regulations, Educational Service

84. The command educational service is controlled by the command education officer who is borne on the strength of the command headquarters.

85. The work of the educational service is carried out by education officers who are appointed to the various R.A.F. stations and training establishments.

RAF airmen are issued with their uniforms and equipment.

CHAPTER XV
MAINTENANCE

General Principles

1. Maintenance of air forces in the field denotes the process of supplying them with all the material which they require, but not personnel. The term includes the supervision, direction and control of the organization for the delivery of necessary requirements in the way most suitable to the units of the force. It also includes the repair, overhaul and salvage of unserviceable material and the proper care of the equipment of units.

2. The material required by the forces in the field is divided, for purposes of administration, into various categories, as follows:—

  (i) Material peculiar to the Royal Air Force that is:—
    (a) Aircraft, engines and spares.
    (b) Motor transport and spares.
    (c) Signal, armament and other technical equipment.
    (d) Special tools and materials.
    (e) Special R.A.F. clothing.
  (ii) Aircraft bombs, special types of ammunition, and pyrotechnics.
  (iii) All other stores, including works stores, camp and barrack equipment, tentage, ordinary medical stores and clothing common to the Royal Air Force and the Army; but excluding "supplies" as defined in sub-para. (iv).
  (iv) Supplies, namely food, petrol and lubricants, (both aviation and M.T.), lighting material, disinfectants and medical comforts.

The Control and Execution of Maintenance Duties

3. Maintenance duties are the joint responsibility of and are jointly undertaken by the engineer and equipment services. The administrative branch, organization section, is responsible for the control of the policy of these two services. In matters requiring special technical knowledge which arise in the course of maintenance the policy staff is advised by the heads or representatives of the engineer and equipment services as appropriate.

4. Subject to general direction by the policy staff the heads of the services concerned are responsible for the carrying out of maintenance duties by the units designed for this purpose and supplied from R.A.F. establishments. Ancillary units from other than R.A.F. sources are similarly administered by the heads of their respective services.

The Process of Maintenance

5. The process of maintenance is broadly divisible into seven stages. These are as follows:—
  (i) Design.
  (ii) Provision.

(iii) Production.
(iv) Holding.
 (v) Repairs and overhauls.
(vi) Salvage.
(vii) Distribution.

Design

6. Design is the process of developing a war store from its original conception. It is primarily the concern of home authority, but it is the duty of the forces in the field to put forward, through headquarters, recommendations concerning the design of their existing equipment or proposals for new equipment.

Provision

7. Provision denotes the anticipation of requirements and arrangements in connection with the eventual receipt and utilization. Provision is normally the business of home authority, whose programme, however, is dependent upon the situation of the forces in the field. When provisioning arrangements are being made, both prior to and during a campaign, the following factors must be taken into consideration:—

 (i) The rate of consumption by the forces in the field.
 (ii) The extent to which the material consumed can be replaced from material repaired or overhauled in the field.
(iii) The reserves of material to be held in the theatre of war, including working and transit stocks.
(iv) The special characteristics of the campaign which affect consumption or call for provision of material, e.g. enemy air action against base areas, tropical climate, or unfavourable flying conditions.

Performing maintenance on an aircraft undercarriage.

Production

8. Production is the process by which requirements are obtained; viz. by requisition, purchase, or manufacture. The process includes testing and inspection before issue and also delivery from the original source to the Royal Air Force. Production is normally the responsibility of home authority, but in special circumstances may be delegated to an overseas command or made the subject of special arrangements in the theatre of war.

Reserve of Material

9. The reserves of material to be held in the theatre of war must be decided after careful consideration of the following factors:—

(i) The normal rate at which replacements and supplies will be required by the units in the field, taking into account the special characteristics of the campaign.

(ii) The possibility of the occurrence of emergency demands over and above the normal.

(iii) The extent to which demands can be met from material repaired and overhauled in the field.

(iv) The conditions of transportation to and from the theatre of the war and the possibility of interruption of the lines of communication.

10. The A.O.C.-in-C. will review, periodically throughout the campaign, the adequacy of the reserves of material. He will ensure also that no unnecessary stock of material is allowed to impair the efficiency or mobility of units.

11. Reserves of stores liable to deterioration must be administered in a way that ensures a turnover of the individual items.

12. When the storage of reserve material is being arranged, consideration must be given to the relative advantages of the economies in administration effected by storage in large quantities in a few places or the greater security from enemy action obtained by distribution in smaller quantities over a wider area.

13. If in a campaign on a large scale it should be decided to divide the aircraft depot into subsidiary depots with separate functions, stores and repair organizations should normally be in close proximity. This will facilitate rapid transit of unserviceable and other material from store to repair units, and of repaired material from repair depots to store units.

14. Reserves of material are divided into three classes, namely:—

(i) Stores and spares of all types for which the daily requirements of the force can only be estimated on a broad basis, and for which demands ranging over a large number of individual items may be heavy or light for varying periods. Units are allowed an establishment for a certain reserve of these articles, and replacements for items used are obtained by specific indents.

(ii) Supplies, as defined in para. 2, sub-para (iv) above, of which the individual items are limited in number and for which there is a continual but fluctuating daily requirement depending on certain definite factors, such as number of hours flown by aircraft, mileage covered by M.T. or intensity of air fighting. Units obtain supplies on indent but do not normally hold a considerable reserve.

(iii) Ammunition and bombs, for which indents are not submitted by units. The daily expenditure of these items by units is replaced automatically by higher authority on notification of that expenditure.

Reserves of Stores and Spares

15. A reserve of stores and spares forms part of the equipment of the fighting units. The amount of this reserve is normally two to three days' requirements, but this in special circumstances may be modified. A further reserve of stores and spares, excluding complete aircraft, is held by the air stores parks. This reserve normally represents another thirty days' requirements. The remaining reserves and all reserve aircraft are held by the aircraft or other depots, according to an establishment fixed in accordance with para. 9 above. The principles upon which are based the reserves of aircraft and engines are given in paragraphs 17 to 23 below.

Reserves of Supplies and Ammunition

16. The main reserves of supplies and ammunition are held in depots. Owing to the bulky nature of supplies and the vulnerable nature of ammunition and fuel, only a limited amount of these commodities is held by units. A definite amount of supplies and ammunition is normally in transit between depots and units, and this may be regarded as a further reserve. In principle, in addition to the complete or partly expended day's requirements held at units, there will also be two days' full supplies in transit between the railhead and the unit. This two days' supply may in certain circumstances be kept on wheels, or may be dumped at a convenient place.

RAF ground crew install ammunition belts into a Fairey Battle.

Reserves of aircraft in the field

17. The reserves of aircraft to be maintained in the field must include:—

(i) An effective reserve from which replacements may be made to the fighting units.
(ii) A non-effective reserve or "working stock" to cover aircraft under repair or in transit.

18. An estimate of aircraft consumption must be made before the amount of the reserves can be decided. In making this estimate an important factor is the number of hours flown, but it is also affected by special factors such as:—

(i) The intensity of air fighting;
(ii) The suitability of aerodromes in use; or
(iii) The nature of the country for forced landings.

19. In addition to allowing for these factors, in order to arrive at the probable number of replacement aircraft required within a given period by a unit, it is necessary to estimate:—

(i) The total number of hours' flying that may be carried out in that period.
(ii) The average number of hours that will be flown for each replacement effected.

Statistics are published annually which give these figures under the conditions met with in various spheres of activity of the Royal Air Force, but forecasts of probable wastage should, if possible, be made by the air branch from time to time.

20. The reserves of aircraft in the field must also include a margin to maintain supplies in event of transportation difficulties affecting the flow of reserves from home establishment.

Reserves of engines in the field

21. All aircraft in the theatre of war, whether in units in reserve or as airframes, must have an engine either installed or available for them. The engine reserves must therefore be based upon the same factors as the reserves of aircraft. In addition to the engines in initial equipment and effective reserve aircraft, there are also required engines to cover those of necessity non-effective at any one time. These non-effective engines include:—

(i) Those held in maintenance units earmarked for squadrons.
(ii) The working stock in maintenance units. 25 per cent. of the squadrons' establishment of engines will be held by air stores parks. The working stock behind squadrons depends upon the conditions and the repair programme in the theatre of war. It is further affected by the particular type of engine concerned and the frequency of the overhauls required by the engine.

Repairs and Overhauls

22. Prior to the commencement of a campaign, the Air Ministry, in consultation with the air force commander, must decide upon the programme of repairs and overhauls to aircraft, engines, M.T., and other material in the field. The following factors must be taken into consideration before the programme is decided:—

(i) The capacity of the fighting units for repair and overhaul of their material. This depends upon the intensity of the operations they will be called upon to carry out and the facilities at the disposal of units. As regards aircraft, fighting units should not be called upon to undertake such repairs as they are likely seriously to impair the fighting efficiency of the unit whilst they are being carried out.

(ii) The extent to which adequate facilities can be provided in the field at depots for large scale repairs and overhauls, and the time which must elapse before these facilities are available.

Ground crew remove an engine cowling to make essential maintenance.

(iii) The facilities of transportation in, to and from the theatre of war and its distance from home.

(iv) The availability of overhaul and repair facilities in other overseas commands.

23. When the programme policy has been decided, the establishment of the depots should then be settled. The efficiency of the repair organization is greatly impaired by interference with its programme once it has been put into operation. When, therefore, the repair programme has been put into operation, it must be realized that any change can only become effective after a considerable lapse of time.

Salvage

24. When any aircraft is damaged beyond the capacity of the unit to repair, the officer commanding the unit will take action in accordance with the separate special instructions referred to in para. 33. He will then be informed by signal whether the aircraft is to be:—

(i) Returned as a whole to a depot.

(ii) Abandoned or burnt after removal of certain scheduled components and items of equipment.

(iii) Dealt with in any special way.

25. The actual salvage of crashes may be carried out by the appropriate fighting unit or by the salvage sections controlled at home by Maintenance Command and abroad or in the field by the maintenance organization. The advantage of salvage being a responsibility of the maintenance organization is that it is carried out with greater care and efficiency, losses are less likely to occur, and aircraft can be salvaged irrespective of the movement or employment of the fighting units.

Distribution

26. Distribution means the allocation and issue of replenishments to the forces in the field. The policy of distribution is the responsibility of the staff. The machinery for meeting the demands of units in accordance with this policy is provided by the units of the maintenance organization. The transportation of the material involved from one place to another is controlled by the movement section of the staff and is carried out by the appropriate transport or transportation service.

27. Units make known their requirements for material, except bombs and ammunition, by means of demands. These are submitted for the various categories of articles in accordance with the procedure laid down in the separate special instruction referred to in para. 33. They may be submitted for normal day to day requirements or, in respect of material required in considerable quantities, from time to time, either for the purpose of carrying out special work, for replenishment, or for the creation of dumps. As regards bombs and ammunition, see paragraph 14, sub-paragraph (iii) above.

28. Requirements which can be foreseen and normal replacements will be supplied as a matter of routine by the air stores parks in the theatre of operations to which the demand is sent. Air stores parks will maintain their authorized stocks by demands upon the aircraft depot. When, however, demands occur for special items, or to an extent seriously affecting the stocks of the aircraft or other depot, either in quantity or description, the demand will be referred by the depot receiving it to higher authority.

29. Units will apply for replacements of aircraft by signal, through their formation headquarters. Air Headquarters will allot aircraft through the maintenance organization, which, on being notified of the numbers of aircraft allotted, will detail the machines and arrange for their delivery.

30. Commanding Officers submitting demands are always responsible for ensuring that material is demanded in accordance with regulations and is only demanded to bring material in possession of units up to the authorized scale. The authority responsible for the issue of material in compliance with a demand is responsible for the examination of the demand with a view to ensuring economy.

A pilot, still in full flying gear, converses with a member of the WAAF.

CHAPTER 5
THE CHANGING BATTLE

The introduction at the beginning of this book provided an outline of the Battle of Britain. Historical hindsight does us the favour of presenting a complete narrative of the battle from beginning to end; we know the outcome from the moment we start reading. The following documents therefore serve as a useful reminder that for those who fought the campaign, endings were not seen, rather the battle evolved across days, weeks and months, with endless oscillations in fortune making the future hard to predict.

Both of the documents here come from the pen of Keith Park, the commander of No. 11 Group. The first is an instruction to Group Controllers and Sector Commanders on 19 August 1940, informing them of the shift in German strategy and how they should adjust their procedures accordingly. The second is an official report on the air combat from 8 August to 10 September 1940, a period that largely decided the outcome of the battle. The terse, formal language of both texts masks a furious human drama. In total, the Battle of Britain cost the lives of 1,542 RAF and 2,550 Luftwaffe aircrew. Total aircraft losses were 1,744 for the RAF and 1,977 for the Luftwaffe. We can add to these sober numbers the deaths of the ground crew mentioned in the previous chapter, plus c. 14,300 civilians killed and more than 20,000 injured in bombing raids. The Battle of Britain may today be lauded as a seminal British victory, and a resounding moment in Britain's cultural identity, but the outcome that we know must never overshadow the price paid by those whose horizons were purely on the day ahead of them.

From 'No 11 Group Instructions to Controllers. No.4' (1940)
SECRET

No 11 GROUP INSTRUCTIONS TO CONTROLLERS. No 4

From: Air Officer Commanding, No 11 Group, Royal Air Force.
To: Group Controllers and Sector Commanders, for Sector Controllers.
Date: 19 August 1940.

The German Air Force has begun a new phase in air attacks, which have been switched from coastal shipping and ports on to inland objectives. The bombing attacks have for several days been concentrated against aerodromes, and especially fighter aerodromes, on the coast and inland. The following instructions are issued to meet the changed conditions:

a) Despatch fighters to engage large enemy formations over land or within gliding distance of the coast. During the next two or three weeks, we cannot afford to lose pilots through forced landings in the sea;
b) Avoid sending fighters out over the sea to chase reconnaissance aircraft or small formations of enemy fighters;
c) Despatch a pair of fighters to intercept single reconnaissance aircraft that come inland. If clouds are favourable, put a patrol of one or two fighters over an aerodrome which enemy aircraft are approaching in clouds;
d) Against mass attacks coming inland, despatch a minimum number of squadrons to engage enemy fighters. Our main object is to engage enemy bombers, particularly those approaching in cloud layer;
e) If all our Squadrons around London are off the ground engaging enemy mass attacks, ask 12 Group or Command Controller to provide squadrons to patrol aerodromes Debden, North Weald, Hornchurch;
f) If heavy attacks have crossed the coast and are proceeding towards aerodromes, put a Squadron, or even the Sector Training Flight, to patrol under clouds over each Sector aerodrome;
g) 303 (Polish) Squadron can provide two sections for patrol of inland aerodromes, especially while the older Squadrons are on the ground refuelling, when enemy formations are flying over land;
h) 1 (Canadian) Squadron can be used in the same manner by day as other fighter squadrons.

(Sgd) K.R. Park
Air Vice-Marshal,
Commanding, No 11
Royal Air Force

A formation of Ju 87 Stuka dive-bombers.

From 'German Air Attacks on England' (1940)

German Air Attacks on England. – 8th Aug. – 10th Sept.

As directed in your letter FC/S.21069/Air, dated 6th September, 1940, I have to submit the following brief report on operations in No.11 Group area since the German offensive began on August 8th, 1940. As the battle still continues unabated by day, and has increased greatly in intensity by night, neither I nor any of my Staff have opportunity to write a lengthy report.

2. The appended report covers the period from 8th August to 10th September, during which there were three distinct phases in which the enemy altered his plan and tactics. The first phase was from 8th August to 18th August, and the second phase was from 19th August to 5th September. The 6th September began a third phase, which is now occupying all my Group's attention by day and by night.

FIRST PHASE – 8th August to 18th August, 1940:

Enemy Strategy:

3. Bombing attacks were directed against the following objectives:-

a) Shipping and ports on the South-East and South coast, between North Foreland and Portland;

b) Massed attacks against Portland and Portsmouth;

c) Attacks on fighter aerodromes on the coast, followed by Bomber Command and Coastal Command aerodromes on the coast;

d) Towards the end of this period, comparatively light attacks were pressed inland by day to various objectives.

Enemy Tactics:

4. To employ massed formations of bombers, escorted by massed formations of single-engine and twin-engine fighters. The bombing attacks were mostly medium or high dive-bombing. Dive bombers, Ju.87s, were used extensively, and also in lesser numbers, He.111, Do.17 and Ju.88. As this phase progressed, the enemy diverted the weight of his attack from shipping and ports on to aerodromes on the coast and R.D.F. Stations. Night attacks began to grow during this period, attacks by a number of single aircraft being made inland to various objectives.

Method of Attack:

5. The enemy usually made an attack against coastal objectives in Kent as a diversion in order to draw our fighters, then about thirty to forty minutes later, put in his main attack against ports or aerodromes on the South coast between Brighton and Portland.

6. This phase introduced bombing by Me.110s and also 109s. Me.109s also carried out machinegun attacks on forward aerodromes.

Tactics of Enemy Fighter Cover:

7. During this phase the unwieldy mass formations, usually 10,000 feet – about the bombers. These tactics were not very effective in protecting the bombers.

Employment of Our Fighters:

8. The main problem was to know which was the diversionary attack and to hold sufficient fighter squadrons in readiness to meet the main attack when this could be discerned from the very unreliable information received from the R.D.F., after they had been heavily bombed. To meet these attacks on coastal objectives, it was essential to keep nearly all Readiness squadrons at forward aerodromes, such as Lympne, Hawkinge, Manston, Rochford. The greatest vigilance had to be observed by Group Controller not to have these squadrons bombed or machinegunned on the ground at forward aerodromes. On only one occasion was any squadron at a forward aerodrome attacked while on the ground refuelling, and this was because the squadron failed to maintain a protective patrol over the base during refuelling.

9. A very high state of preparedness had to be maintained in order to engage the enemy before he reached his coastal objectives. The general plan in employing the fighters was to detail about half the available squadrons, including the Spitfires, to engage the enemy fighters, and the remainder to attack the enemy bombers, which normally flew at between 11,000 and 13,000 feet, and carried out their attack frequently from 7,000 to 8,000 feet,

Tactics of Our Fighters:

10. During this phase our fighters were mainly employing the Fighter Command attacks from astern. These gave good results against the enemy fighters,

which were unarmoured, but were not so effective against the bombers. Our fighters were therefore advised to practice deflection shots from quarter astern, also from above end from below against twin-engine bombers.

Volume of Flying by Fighter Squadrons:

11. During this phase, fighter squadrons not infrequently flew over fifty hours each in one day with twelve aircraft in commission.

Casualties:

12. The casualties to pilots and aircraft were about equal in numbers for any given engagement. Owing to the lack of trained formation and Section leaders, also to the fitting of armour to enemy bombers, our casualties were relatively higher than during May and June, when operating over France and Belgium.

Results of Air Combat:

13. Results were satisfactory, the proportion of enemy shot down to our own losses being about four to one, slightly below the average when fighting over France. As much of this fighting took place over the sea, casualties were higher than they would have been if the fighting had been over land. The results of air combat were good because the enemy fighters were frequently too high to protect their bombers. Moreover, the Ju.87 proved an easy prey to both Hurricanes and Spitfires.

Conclusion:

14. It would appear that our fighter defences proved too good for the enemy, because on August 18th the Germans withdrew their dive bombers, Ju.87s, and there was a break of five days in intensive operations.

SECOND PHASE – 19th August to 5th September, 1940:

Enemy Strategy:

15. With this phase, enemy attacks began to turn to:

a) Inland aerodromes and aircraft factories;
b) Industrial targets and areas which could only be classified as residential.

Attacks by day to the West of Sussex diminished markedly during this period, and greatly increased over Kent, Thames Estuary and Essex.

Enemy Tactics:

16. Possibly owing to the increased range of targets, to heavy losses which had been experienced, or to the wish to conserve them for other tasks, dive-bombing by Ju.87s was not employed during this period. Night attacks greatly increased in strength.

Method of Attack:

17. During this period the enemy modified his diversionary attacks against different parts of the country, presumably for the reasons that he had not found this method to pay – or because he had not the forces to spare. His attacks were, however, made on a wider front using a greater number of very high fighter screens and smaller bomber formations.

Tactics of Enemy Fighter Cover:

18. Some formations of long range bombers have been boxed in by close fighter escorts, some of which flew slightly above to a flank or in rear, others slightly above and ahead, with a third lot of fighters weaving between the sub-formations of bombers. On several occasions raids of this type barged through our first and second screen of fighters and reached their objectives by sheer weight of numbers, even after having suffered numerous casualties to stragglers and flank sub-formations. On several occasions, smallish formations of long range bombers deliberately left their fighter escort immediately it was engaged by our fighters, and, losing height, proceeded towards objectives in the South or South-West of London without any close fighter escort. Most of these raids were engaged by our rear rank of fighters, either when about to bomb or when retreating, and suffered heavy casualties.

Employment of Our Fighters:

19. As the enemy penetrated further inland, we adopted the tactics of meeting the enemy formations in pairs of squadrons, while calling on Nos. 10 and 12 Groups to provide close cover for our aerodromes near London and for suburban aircraft factories West of London. This arrangement enabled us to meet the enemy further forward in greater strength while giving a measure of close protection against enemy raids which might elude us at various heights.

20. On some occasions it therefore became practicable to detail a wing of two Spitfire squadrons to engage escorting enemy fighters, while a wing of Hurricanes engaged the bombers.

21. The use of Hawkinge and Manston became rarer during this period, owing to the heavy scale of attack to which they were subjected, and the fact that squadrons were required to go into action in pairs and were consequently based together at inland aerodromes.

Volume of Flying by Fighter Squadrons:

22. To ease the load on squadrons the close escort of convoys was abolished, except for the unlikely event of a day passage between North Foreland and Dungeness. The flying hours therefore did not rise materially per day.

Casualties:

23. The heavy fighting much depleted many squadrons, and a number were withdrawn (and sometimes their ground personnel as well), for rest and training of new pilots, their places being taken by fresh squadrons from Northern Groups which had been comparatively inactive. It was again very noticeable that the heaviest casualties were experienced in the newly arrived squadrons, in spite of their being strong in numbers.

Results of Combats:

24. Results of combats were numerically satisfactory, although the enemy escort fighters engaged more closely and so reduced the number of enemy bombers turned back or shot down. Moreover, the latter were increasingly heavily armoured and in greater strength, also better handled than previously. The employment of more heavily armoured and armed bombers resulted in our casualties to pilots being high, and wastage in aircraft being very heavy.

THIRD PHASE – 6th September, onwards:

Enemy Strategy:

25. On Saturday, September 7th, the enemy first turned to the heavy attack of London by day – perhaps because his timetable called for it, or because his Intelligence staff was persuaded (on the example of Poland) that our fighter defence was sufficiently weakened by the previous month's attacks. This change of bombing plan saved 11 Group Sector Stations from becoming inoperative and enabled them to carry on operations, though at a much lower standard of efficiency.

Enemy Tactics:

26. Dive bombers reappeared in attacks on coastal objectives and shipping off Essex and Kent. These attacks were made under cover of massed attacks by long range bombers against inland objectives. Enemy attacks on inland objectives were made in two or three distinct waves, following one another at about twenty minute intervals, the whole attack lasting up to one hour. Each wave has consisted of a number of raids of from twenty to forty bombers having an equal number of fighters in close escort, and covered at a much higher altitude by large formations of other fighters. The majority of the raids were at higher altitude, above 15,000 feet, in bright sunlit skies that made it practically impossible for the Observer Corps to give accurate information as to the strength or type of the enemy formations flying overhead.

Method of Attack:

27. The attack of September 7th was pressed home by the weight and numbers of successive waves of bombers at short intervals, mainly with fighter escort, all directed at the London area, and in particular at the Docks.

28. Heavy concentrations of attacks by large numbers of single aircraft, followed the day attacks. These methods of attack have been followed on September 9th and 11th, when the sky was sufficiently clear of clouds. Up to the present, the subsequent attacks have not penetrated so well or done so much damage as on September 7th, and enemy losses have been consistently heavy. On 11th September, the enemy carried out a simultaneous attack on Southampton with fifty or sixty aircraft. The greater damage has probably been done by night raids, in which all pretence of attacking military objectives has been abandoned and consists mainly in [unintelligible] the huge London target.

Tactics of Enemy Fighter Cover:
29. Some formations of fighters have been used to make very high diversionary raids in advance of bombers having close escort.

Contrails and battle smoke lace the summer sky of southern England during the Battle of Britain.

Employment of Our Fighters:
30. We have developed during this phase an arrangement to engage the first wave of a large raid with six Readiness squadrons (Spitfires high, and Hurricanes for bombers) in pairs; to hold about eight Squadrons to meet the second wave half way to the coast; for the remaining squadrons to cover aircraft factories and aerodromes, or if necessary to be thrown in to meet a third wave; leaving Nos. 10 and 12 Group squadrons to cover I Sector aerodromes North and West and aircraft factories. On the 9th and 11th of September, these new dispositions were very successful. Out of twenty-one squadrons of No.11 Group despatched, nineteen engaged, inflicting heavy losses on the enemy. In spite of this, however, one heavy raid of about forty to fifty bombers broke through and reached Eastern London before effectively being attacked by our fighters.

31. To increase the proportion of engagement, despite the handicaps of R.D.F. inaccuracy on aircraft at great height, various observer corps failures, damage to G.P.O, lines and temporary partial dislocation by the movement of Sector Operations Rooms, it was decided to employ a single V.H.F. Spitfire to shadow enemy raids, and report to Sectors, who report to Group. The results so far have not shown what value this will prove to the air defences.

32. A further temporary handicap on the employment of our fighters has been the measures taken against bombing attacks to disperse non-essential administrative, etc., personnel and equipment away from Sector Stations. This is a matter which is clearing itself rapidly now, and will eventually lead to decreased vulnerability to enemy air attack.

Volume of Flying by Fighter Squadrons:

33. No increase in this phase as yet.

Casualties:

34. It has been decided, for the present, not to replace squadrons which have been hammered, but to keep them filled up to a minimum of sixteen operationally trained pilots by transfers from Northern Groups which, being less heavily engaged and being more remote from the area of combat, are able to train new pilots from O.T.U.s up to operational standard. The wastage in Hurricanes has been unduly heavy owing to the many instances of gravity tanks being set on fire in in combat. Attention was drawn to this and recommendations made to Command Headquarters some weeks ago.

Results of Air Combat:

35. Despite the heavy armouring of enemy bombers, our more highly developed tactics of concentration and interception, the adoption of head on also beam attacks, has enabled us to inflict a heavier proportion of losses during this period than during the second phase under report.

Effect of Bombing Attacks on Fighter Aerodromes:

36. Contrary to general belief and official reports, the enemy's bombing attacks by day did extensive damage to five of our forward aerodromes and also to six of our seven Sector Stations. The damage to forward aerodromes was so severe that Manston and Lympne were on several occasions for days quite unfit for operating fighters.

37. Biggin Hill was so severely damaged that only one squadron could operate from there and the remaining two squadrons had to be placed under the control of adjacent Sectors for over a week. Had the enemy continued his heavy attacks against the adjacent Sectors and knocked out their Operations Rooms or telephone communications, the fighter defences of London would have been in a parlous state

during the last critical phase when heavy attacks have been directed against the capital.

38. Sector Operations Rooms have on three occasions been put out of action, either by direct hits or by damage to G.P.O. cables, and all Sectors took into use their Emergency Operations Rooms, which were not only too small to house the essential personnel, but had never been provided with the proper scale of G.P.O. landlines to enable normal operation of three squadrons per Sector. In view of this grave deficiency, arrangements were made to establish alternative Sector Operations Rooms within five miles of each Sector aerodrome, and this work is now proceeding on the highest priority.

39. At several important aerodromes and Sectors, enemy bombing put out of action the Stations organization by destroying telephone communications, buildings, etc. Fortunately, the enemy switched his raids from aerodromes on to industrial and other objectives, and gave a short respite during which the Station organization at bombed aerodromes was completely reorganized.

40. The attacks on our fighter aerodromes soon proved that the Air Ministry's arrangements for labour and equipment quickly to repair aerodrome surfaces were absolutely inadequate, and this has been made the subject of numerous signals and letters during the past four weeks.

41. There was a critical period between 28th August and 5th September when the damage to Sector Stations and our ground organization was having a serious effect on the fighting efficiency of the fighter squadrons, who could not be given the same good technical and administrative service as previously. As a result of an immense amount of hard work day and night on the part of Group Staff and personnel at Sector Stations and satellite aerodromes, the critical period was tided over, without any interruption in the operations of our fighter squadrons. The absence of many essential telephone lines, the use of scratch equipment in emergency Operations Rooms, and the general dislocation of ground organization, was seriously felt for about a week in the handling of squadrons by day to meet the enemy's massed attacks, which were continued without the former occasional break of a day.

Conclusion:

42. At the time of writing, confidence is felt in our ability to hold the enemy by day and to prevent his obtaining superiority in the air over our territory, unless he greatly increases the scale or intensity of his attacks. Every endeavour is now being made to improve our fighter defences by night. To achieve this aim will require not only better equipment, but greater specialisation of pilots on night flying and fighting.

K.R. Park
Air Vice-Marshal, Commanding,
No.11 Group, Royal Air Force

SOURCES

INTRODUCTION

AIR 9-132-2, National Archives, 'Measures to be taken to ensure co-ordination of action in the event of a German invasion of England' (1939)

CHAPTER 1

Air Ministry, *Royal Air Force War Manual, Part 2, Organization and Administration*, 2nd edition (1940)

Air Ministry, *Handbook of the German Air Force* (1939)

US War Department, *Handbook on German Military Forces*, TME-30-451 (1945)

CHAPTER 2

Air Ministry, *Royal Air Force War Manual, Part 1, Operations*, 2nd edition (1940)

Air Ministry, *Royal Air Force War Manual, Part 2, Organization and Administration*, 2nd edition (1940)

Air Ministry, *Instructions for Observer Posts* (1941)

US Navy, *40 MM Antiaircraft Gun*, OP 820, Department of Ordnance (1943)

CHAPTER 3

Sailor Malan, 'Ten of My Rules for Air Fighting' (1940)

Air Ministry, 'Hints and Tips for Fighter Pilots', Air Tactics Branch (1940)

AIR 14/157, National Archives, 'Enemy Fighter Tactics' (1940)

AIR 14/2786, National Archives, 'Tactical information gained from German Air Force attacks on R.A.F. Aerodromes' (1940)

AIR 16/274, National Archives, 'Fighter Tactics' (1940)

AIR 16/282, National Archives, 'Tactics for Fighters v German Formations' (1940)

AIR 16/334, National Archives, 'Fighters versus Fighters' (1940)

AIR 16/334, National Archives, 'Fighter Command Tactical Memorandum No.5' (1939)

AIR 16/334, National Archives, 'Fighter Command Tactical Memorandum No.7' (1940)

AIR 16/375, National Archives, 'No.12 Group Operation Instruction no. Reinforcement of No.11 Group' (1940)

AIR 16/375, National Archives, 'Use of Wing Formations against Present Enemy Tactics' (1940)

AIR 20/2079, National Archives, 'Air Staff Note on the Operation of Fighter Wings' (1940)

Air Ministry, *Pilot's Notes: Spitfire IIA and IIB Aeroplanes Merlin XII Engine* (1940)

CHAPTER 4

Air Ministry, *Royal Air Force War Manual, Part 2, Organization and Administration*, 2nd edition (1940)

CHAPTER 5

Keith Park, 'No 11 Group Instructions to Controllers. No.4 (1940)
AIR 16/635-4A, National Archives, 'German Air Attacks on England' (1940)